Following the Call of Jesus

A Sermon Series on the Book of Ephesians

David Ratcliff

$\mathcal{C}_{\mathcal{D}}$

Parson's Porch Books

www.parsonsporchbooks.com

Following the Call of Jesus: A Sermon Series on the Book of Ephesians

ISBN: Softcover 978-1-951472-36-8

Copyright © 2020 by David Ratcliff

I dedicate this book to:

*the community of faith at Shepherd of the Sierra
Presbyterian Church who have faithfully listened and
embodied the gospel throughout our years together and
to the memory of a dear colleague, Kent Milton, whose
vision and editorial eye made this book possible.*

Contents

Introduction

I was 19 years old when I delivered my first sermon. The year was 1976 and unbeknownst to me there were ongoing scholarly debates as to the future of preaching within the American context. The power of media, the lowering attention span of most people, and the growing sense that the very act of people gathering to hear someone speak for an extended amount of time seemed at best passé.

Very little of those concerns have changed over the past forty years. In fact, in many ways those concerns have increased as we continue to be influenced by the lightening pace of modern technology. And yet, the act of preaching continues to have a place of relevance in our churches. While the ways in which preaching is practiced vary greatly, there remains the fundamental reality that preaching still matters.

I am deeply grateful for that reality. Preaching remains a central part of who I am as a pastor; it continues to both challenge and humble me. The act of standing before a congregation and sharing the Good News of the gospel remains one of the most important acts I do within the context of ministry.

I am a strong believer that all sermons are deeply contextual. Effective sermons are rooted in a particular community, shared within a particular time, and heard within a unique set of human circumstances. Thus the very act of publishing a set of sermons raises a number of problems. Will these words have life apart from the community in which they were birthed? Can a message live apart from the particular time it was first delivered? Can the words which were given within a particular time and place be heard again within other contexts?

I do not have good answers for any of these questions. I simply know that as I bring these sermons together in this brief book, such questions must be acknowledged. It is my hope that an affirmative "Yes" can be given to each, but only time will tell.

The following sermons were given in the fall of 2018 at Shepherd of the Sierra Presbyterian Church. I have been privileged to pastor Shepherd since 1995. These words have been transcribed from my oral delivery. My congregation is aware that I do not preach from a manuscript, nor do I use notes. While this mode of delivery works on any given Sunday, it does offer unique challenges for the written word. It does not take long for the eye of the reader to notice that oral speech differs in its cadence and phrasing. The text of these sermons has been altered some to allow for a smoother read (for this I am deeply thankful to my wife, Deb Aucoin-Ratcliff), but the feel and cadence of the words reflect the oral form in which they were originally shared.

It is my hope that those who take the time to read one or more of these sermons will be able to hear the truth of each message, even though the words are no longer tied to a particular time and place that was found in Loomis, California from September to November, 2018. I believe that the truth of God's message to the world is one that can transcend time and place. It is my prayer that God's Spirit will be faithful in opening your heart to the truth of these once spoken words and that they may have a new life within the context of a book.

Chapter 1

Living A Blessed Life

Introduction

I think everyone has passages from Scripture that are foundational in their life of faith. The Book of Ephesians has become just such a book for me. While at times the book can be quite dense, there are so many other times when this epistle offers windows of divine understanding that truly color the way I look at life.

In this opening section of the book, Paul offers a blessing over the people (I am very aware of the scholarly debate concerning Pauline authorship. Having read many opinions on this matter, I am comfortable asserting Paul as its author). The act of blessing someone is not all that common in our culture. We may bless our food before each meal, but the act of offering a blessing over an individual is rare.

This opening sermon will seek to focus on not only the content of Paul's blessing but the very act of blessing. It is my hope that in hearing Paul's call to acknowledge the fact that we are a blessed people, we can in turn offer God's blessings to those around us.

Scripture: Ephesians 1:3-14

"Blessed be the God and Father of our Lord Jesus Christ, who has blessed us in Christ with every spiritual blessing in the heavenly places, just as he chose us in Christ before the foundation of the world to be holy and blameless before him in love. He destined us for adoption as his children through

Jesus Christ, according to the good pleasure of his will, to the praises of his glorious grace that he freely bestowed on us in the Beloved. In him we have redemption through his blood, the forgiveness of our trespasses, according to the riches of his grace that he lavished on us. With all wisdom and insight he has made known to us the mystery of his will, according to his good pleasure that he set forth in Christ, as a plan for the fullness of time, to gather up all things in him, things in heaven and things on earth. In Christ we have also obtained an inheritance, having been destined according to the purpose of him who accomplishes all things according to his counsel and will, so that we, who were the first to set our hope in Christ, might live for the praise of his glory. In him you also, when you had heard the word of truth, the gospel of your salvation, and had believed in him, were marked with the seal of the promised Holy Spirit; this is the pledge of our inheritance toward redemption as God's own people, to the praise of his glory" (Ephesians 1:3-14, NRSV).

Sermon

Today we begin a 11-week journey through the book of Ephesians. Ephesians has been a fundamental book in my own life journey. This thick file folder I am holding is overstuffed with notes on the Book of Ephesians. As you look more closely at this file it appears quite gnarly. I've got lots of notes; I've got things that indicate the datedness of this file. For example, here's a teaching tool many of you haven't used in a while…the good ol' overhead transparency. But what really surprised me about this file was something I had totally lost track of…it's a 4-page, typed document called "A prospectus for a class on the book of Ephesians". It's dated April 25, 1983, and it's written to the Christian Education Committee of Calvary Presbyterian Church in San Francisco.

I was pretty impressed with the fact that I typed a four-page document just to get permission to lead the class. But the other thing that struck me is that this is about the time I became a Presbyterian. In many ways it was like saying to my future denominational home, "If you want to know who I am, let me teach you the book of Ephesians." Through this prospectus I was articulating who I am, who I've become, and who I continue to be. Luckily the Calvary Presbyterians granted me permission to type my application, because my handwriting has never been good, but as I look at this manuscript now, I don't think my typing was much better. The pages are filled with all sorts of uncorrected typos, and in many places I just "penned in" corrections to cover over the mistakes I made.

I've always found the book of Ephesians to be a bit maddening, sometimes a bit opaque, and other times vivid, awe inspiring, and very practical. I think it's all of these. As we journey through the coming 11 weeks, I'm hoping that you capture some of those feelings, as well as discovering the reason I think this is such an important book for us to take a look at.

We begin with Ephesians 1:3-14. While not formally a prayer, these verses have the posture of a prayer because Paul is offering a word of blessing over this congregation. Now, one of the maddening things about Ephesians is that occasionally it can pose some obstacles that are a little difficult to get through. In the original Greek text, verses 3-14 compose one sentence. In the New Revised Standard Version, it comprises *six* sentences, So the translators decided that they were going to need six English sentences to help us understand one gargantuan sentence written by Paul.

I love the note of one biblical scholar who said the following about those verses: "This statement is the most monstrous sentence conglomeration I've ever met in the Greek language" (Agnostos Theos, as cited by Marcus Barth in his commentary, p. 77). He's right, it's a mess. But one advantage of looking at the Greek text is that we become aware the sentence has only one main verb, and that verb is *eulogetos*, which means "blessing" or "blessed."

This prayer is all about blessing: God blessing us, and God's people giving praise for that blessing. It's as if Paul is saying "if you want to understand the Christian faith you need to approach it in a posture of prayer that begins with the recognition that God is blessing us." It is the theme of blessing that we will develop further this morning, as well as in future sermons.

This idea of beginning a prayer with blessings is something that Paul would be very familiar with. Many of you may remember that Paul was raised by a Jewish mother. And there's a Jewish prayer called the *berakot*: "Blessed are you, O Lord our God." That prayer continues by listing the reasons we are blessed. This likely was a prayer Paul would have heard when he was a young child; and a prayer he may have even used in the contemporary worship service of first century Palestine. The *berakot* is a way of naming the things that God has done for us that indicate we are a blessed people. There are a number of blessings in this text, but I am only going to explore three.

We begin with the first blessing, which is a blessing of choosing. Paul says God has blessed us because God has chosen us. God has destined us from before the beginning of creation. There is a certain eternal quality to this first blessing; it's as if Paul says, "when you think about God, you cannot help but think that God is one who blesses people by the act of choosing them." And he goes on to say not only are we chosen, but that our 'chosen-ness' is in love: God has chosen us in God's love.

This blessing that we offer to God is indicative of a God who is not a cold, calculating, distant despot, but a very caring God. Marcus Barth summarizes it well in his commentary when he says, "This is not a grim Lord watching over the execution of his predetermined plan, but a smiling Father. He enjoys imparting his riches to many children" (Barth, p. 81). So, this prayer begins with an acknowledgement that God has blessed us by choosing us in love as a loving parent.

Unfortunately, we Christians, and I have to say we Calvinists in particular, have sort of messed this thought up a little bit. I'm sure some of you, when you heard the words, "we were destined" or "we've been chosen" went to certain places in your head labeled *danger* or *trouble*, because many Christians have taken these statements which should be affirming, which should be praising God, and have over-analyzed it, broken them down, trying to figure out God's choices. Namely: who is on the inside, who is on the outside; is it I, is it you, is it both of us, is it someone else? And we've totally missed the fact that all Paul wants us to do is begin the day by saying "We have been blessed by a loving God who has chosen us." *End of story.* And I think we would learn a great deal from this blessing if we just ended with that affirmation.

The second blessing Paul talks about is receiving salvation through Jesus. Paul does not use the actual word "salvation" here. He uses 2 words: forgiveness and redemption- we have received both. Again, I think this is reflective of Paul's Jewish background. Jewish poetry employs parallelism, using two words that have the same meaning, like two sides of the same coin. Paul is saying that God has blessed us by forgiving us and by redeeming us.

I think we all know what forgiveness is…it's the redemption part that we sometimes misunderstand. When the Bible talks about God delivering the people of Israel from the Egyptian captors, culminated by crossing the Red Sea, those actions are called *redemption*. God redeemed the people; in other words, the core meaning of *redemption* is freedom.

Today we know that God also has forgiven us and set us free. How did He do this? He sent Jesus and Jesus' death has allowed us to be forgiven, and that forgiveness was lavishly given. I don't know about you, but most of us have not experienced forgiveness in a lavish kind of way--especially when we receive forgiveness from another human being. How many times have you received forgiveness and then become aware that the act of forgiveness came with strings or footnotes attached? Expectations, things that now must be done, certain reactions that are expected of you, sort of an unwritten contract. In other words, most of us don't, when we're forgiven, suddenly experience that we've been lavished with love and freedom and forgiveness. But when forgiveness is real--lavishly given--the weight is gone, all is new. That's what Paul is trying to convey here. I think we get close to it when we sing *Amazing Grace* and we realize the author is not talking about a grace with added conditions.

The best depiction I have seen of *lavish grace* that portrays real forgiveness and freedom occurs in the movie, *The Mission*. In this film, Robert De Niro plays a former slave trader, Rodrigo Mendoza, who captured natives and enslaved them in central South America. He comes to a point where he wants to change his life. And so he confesses his sins to a priest, Father Gabriel, played by Jeremy Irons. But Father Gabriel realizes that Mendoza needs more than just forgiveness and absolution. He needs to *do* something. So he packs up Mendoza's stuff: his armor and his weapons. He puts them in a large netted container and wraps it with a rope around Mendoza's waist. And then he says to him: "I want you to go back to the village where you used to take slaves and receive their forgiveness."

And so Rodrigo Mendoza climbs up a very steep waterfall--I don't know how he does it, while carrying that heavy weight which is now dangling from his waist. Mendoza finally gets to the top of the falls and then must crawl along the edge of a muddy riverside. When he approaches the village, one of the villagers comes out with a machete and Mendoza knows exactly what's going to happen, he's not going to have his head anymore because these people associate slavery with him. But instead, the man uses the machete to cut off the rope.

It is this scene where the movie becomes so powerful, I can't adequately describe it. All of the weight tumbles down the riverside, into the river, and flows down and eventually cascades over the falls. Mendoza then has this profound sense of release. All the forgiveness and the mercy that were undeserved fill his being and he weeps.

I believe that is what Paul is trying to depict. Jesus brings to all of us an opportunity to receive forgiveness and freedom so lavish that it is incomprehensible for us to understand. It is an awareness that our freedom, that our redemption is a freedom *for*, a freedom *for* service to others. Mendoza becomes a priest and he serves the Indian people until he dies. That is the blessing that we received in Christ.

The third blessing Paul mentions is just going to be a teaser, because he actually talks more about this in Chapter Two. Paul says we have been blessed because God has revealed something in Jesus that has been hidden since the beginning of time. The hint is to be found in the use of pronouns. In the latter part of this prayer he talks about '*us*' and '*you*.' What's going to come about in Chapter Two will be the realization that God's mystery is focused on Gentiles being accepted into God's family.

What is being revealed here is not that we have a God who loves to keep secrets and occasionally share them with people, but rather, a God who has willed forgiveness from the very beginning. It wasn't until Jesus came that we could see what God was trying to do, namely make clear that *all* people are part of God's salvific plan. We have been richly blessed.

Now some of you may think, okay, the pastor's done three points, that sounds like a good ending to a sermon; but I want to go on a little further. It is my hope that every week, as we read through Ephesians, we end the sermon with some practical application; in other words, how do we go home with this material? And so I want to back away from the prayer and make three observations. One is an affirmation, the second is a challenge and the third is a call to a new way of living.

The affirmation in this prayer is that we serve a God who is not a distant uncaring parent-type figure, but someone who is very involved with our life. I love the way Carl Holladay puts it: "The God praised here is not a reclining God, resting on an elbow, surveying the universe in quiet, dispassionate leisure. God is rather seen as one who actively reflects on history and human destiny and does so aggressively, charting purposes and intent even before the beginning of time" (Craddock, p. 66).

What's being depicted here is a God who has come down to us desiring to be a God who saves. This to me fits into that whole emphasis about how we are chosen; we are chosen in love and that love shows that God's choosing is not a cold calculation but rather a very personal, relational, caring for us.

The God we serve is a God who cares for us: a God who has entered into our human condition and knows what we are going through.

The second point is a challenge. When we look at this prayer, when we back away from this prayer, we find that it challenges one of the assumptions that many of us, as Western European Americans have accepted without question: namely that we are independent, autonomous, self-guiding, self-developing persons. In other words, we are captains of our own ships. Blessings don't work if we're captains of our own ships. This prayer seems to say: the world is a gift that God has given us; all that we have is a gift from God. We are not autonomous: in fact we are part of God's family, we're part of the people that God has chosen.

I don't know about you, but sometimes the challenge here is thinking "Did God really choose *that* person?" We can have questions about certain kinds of folks that we may deem unworthy of God's choosing. But I think the real challenge is that on a fairly regular basis, we're fed the line that we are the captains of our own ships; we are captains of our own destiny. We need to pull ourselves up by our own bootstraps and we don't need anybody else's help.

That kind of understanding is so far from the meaning of this prayer. This is a prayer of someone who is not captain of his own ship, but a follower of Jesus who has been richly blessed each and every day by a gracious, loving God. I don't deserve that. God just gives it to me. And I think this is the challenge that we need to continue to work on because the problem with cultural messages is they are so subliminal. It's not until someone challenges these cultural notions that we even realize we've bought into them.

And then, here's my last little take home, and if you've forgotten everything else I've said, this is the one I want you to remember, which is why I've saved it for the last. It's this: that I think this prayer offers us a calling into a new way of life. I'm going to use a really fancy word here. I'll first apologize and then still use it: we are called to be *doxological people*. That is just a fancy way of saying we are a people who ought to praise; who live life in praise. We have been blessed and so we are called to praise. And even further, we are called to enjoy. You know there's nothing worse than a Christian who's looking like they're mad at the world all the time.

Now, I'm not a smiley type, so I'm not talking necessarily about facial features. I'm talking about an attitude toward life. And doxological people's attitude toward life is that, each and every day, we ought to wake up and give praise to God for all that this day is going to offer us. This of course becomes a challenge for me because I am not a morning person and it may take me a good hour or so to really want to praise God in any shape or form.

For others, this is something you can do really easily; you wake up and you just decide what you're going to do and that's praise God. But being a doxological people is more than what we do first thing in the morning. It's the way we approach life, the way we approach the day; it's the way we look at our lives. Are we a people that enjoy being disciples of Jesus? Are we giving praise to a God for what God has done in our lives, and in each and everything that we do?

All of this reminds me of that first question of the larger catechism of the ancient Westminster Confession; it's a bit dated but it's still to the point: "What is the chief end of man?" The answer: "The chief end of man is to glorify God and to enjoy Him forever." Don't work until you're dead. Do not grovel. Don't be sad…ENJOY!!! This is what being a doxological people is and we are in a time and a day when the world needs more doxological people.

I'm not talking about having a happy smile, easily stating that the day is wonderful, the sun is going to come out tomorrow, but rather a deep doxology. Deep praise that says when things are bad, God is even greater. When there's all this negativity, what I want to do is offer praise in a positive way, again not in a flippant kind of way, but at the very core of my being. I have been richly blessed and I want to bless other people. I am blessed by God; I want to bless other people. I think this is something that we need to practice each and every day!

And so I am going to end with a quote from one of my favorite books called *My Grandfather's Blessing*, by Rachael Remen. She writes of an event that happened very early in her life, so it's only a story she's heard from others, but for me, it is one of the most touching stories ever written: "My mother was present at the moment when I met my grandfather. Soon after I was born, she took him to the hospital to see me for the first time in my incubator. She told me that he had stood regarding me in silence through the viewing room window for a long time. I had been very premature. Concerned that he was anxious or even repelled that I was so small and frail, she was about to reassure him when he whispered something under his breath. He had turned to her with a smile and said in Hebrew, 'Blessed art thou, oh Lord our God, King of the universe, who has kept us alive and sustained us, who has brought us whole to this moment.' It was a blessing of gratitude for the gift of life and it was also the beginning of our relationship." (Remen, p. 3)

I know that not all of us have had a wonderful grandfather hovering over our just born self, offering us a blessing. I wish we did. But I want you to know that this text says we have been richly blessed. From the day we were given our first breath until we will breathe no more, God looks over us. Rachael had a grandfather who embodied that truth, praise be to God.

Hopefully some of you sense where my sermon is leading; let's have a few more grandparents and parents offering blessings over children, not to be limited to our own biological children; but over children in general, over our neighbor's, over the people we work with. Let us be a doxological people that offer nothing but blessing and hope and praise in a world that seemingly just wants to grovel in negativity, diatribe, and hostility.

Chapter Sources

Barth, Marcus. <u>Ephesians 1-3.</u> (The Anchor Bible). Garden City, NY: Doubleday and Co. Inc., 1974.

Craddock, Fred, et.al. <u>Preaching Through the Christian Year C</u>. Valley Forge, PA: Trinity Press International, 1994.

Ghia, Fernando; Puttnam, David; Berrando, Maximo (Producers), Joffe, Roland (Director), 1986. <u>The Mission</u>. United Kingdom, Warner Brothers Studios.

Newton, John. "Amazing Grace"

Remen, Rachel N. <u>My Grandfather's Blessings</u>. New York, NY: Riverhead Books. 2000.

Chapter 2

Faith, Power, and Church

Introduction

We live in a world that focuses on the individual and that often makes us question the validity of institutions. In such a context it is hard to hear what Paul says about the church, namely that the church is the body of Christ in the world. This sermon will attempt to challenge the congregation to take Paul's words seriously. It will call us to embrace the reality of being the church, but also to pay attention to what Paul says the church should be.

Scripture: Ephesians 1:15-23

"I have heard of your faith in the Lord Jesus and your love toward all the saints, and for this reason I do not cease to give thanks for you as I remember you in my prayers. I pray that the God of our Lord Jesus Christ, the Father of glory, may give you a spirit of wisdom and revelation as you came to know him, so that, with the eyes of your heart enlightened, you may know what is the hope to which he has called you, what are the riches of his glorious inheritance among the saints, and what is the immeasurable greatness of his power for us who believe, according to the working of his great power. God put this power to work in Christ when he raised him from the dead and seated him at his right hand in the heavenly places, far above all rule and authority and power and dominion, and above every name that is named, not only in this age but also in the age to come. And he has put all things under his feet and has made him the head over all things for the church, which is his body, the fullness of him who fills all in all" (Epheisans 1:15-23, NRSV).

Sermon

It's been my experience in life that when people are confronted with the mystery of God, there seems to be two basic responses. One will be something like St. Francis, a response of silence. St. Francis was attributed to once say, "Share the gospel, and if necessary, use words." Such a perspective represents those who are far more comfortable with silence, quiet, and not saying much. At the opposite end is the Apostle Paul who just seems to write and write and write. Last week we looked at a section of Ephesians where verses 3-14 of chapter 1 were one very long Greek sentence ...I hate to say it, but he's done it again. The whole reading for today is one Greek sentence (1:15-22), and in addition it is filled with all sorts of effusive language. In fact, one person calls Paul a "pleonist." I had to look that word up in the dictionary. I didn't know what 'pleonasm' was. According to the dictionary, pleonasm is the ability to use more words than is necessary. So Paul is truly a pleonist. He uses a lot of words to say just a few things. A good example can be found in verse 19. It's difficult to see Paul's over use of words in English, but in just that little verse Paul uses four different words in Greek for "strength." So there's *dunimis*, from which we get dynamite, *energeitas* from which we get "energy", and *kratus* and *ichous*, which describe human strength. It's like he's looking at the dictionary and thinking, "what more words can I put in here in my attempt to describe this amazing power that God has revealed in Jesus Christ"?

This part of Ephesians is not the easiest to preach on- this is pretty heavy stuff. So, I am going to back away from the text a bit and make three general observations. Hopefully it will give us a sense of where Paul desires to lead us

The first observation is that this whole pleonasm of Paul is because he is trying to describe that which is mystery, that which is beyond comprehension. This mystery centers in the fact that God has shown God's power in Jesus and has raised Him above everything in the universe. Namely, Jesus is Lord of the Cosmos. That is a really difficult concept for modern Presbyterians to think about. Most of us have been taught since the time we were little kids that religion should be lived out "decently and in order." Our faith is small, it's personal, it's private; it's between Jesus and me. Something like when Jesus came down from the cross for my sins, God raised Him from the grave so I can go to heaven, that's the end of the story and life goes on.

In light of that reality Paul somewhat assaults us. He says "No, No, No…in Jesus, God has changed the whole structure of the Cosmos, Jesus is in charge." I enjoy the way Eugene Peterson puts verses 19-23. "All this energy issues from Christ. God raised Him from death and set Him on a throne in deep heaven, in charge of running the universe; everything from galaxies to governments; no name and no power exempt from His rule, and not for just this time being but forever. He is in charge of it all; has the final word on everything. At the center of all of this is Christ, Christ rules the church" (Peterson, p. 2127)

I think that's what Paul is trying to get at; that Christ's resurrection is cosmic in scope. What is interesting is that Paul didn't begin his writings that way. If you notice, he begins very simply, "I have heard of your faithfulness and love for the saints." In other words, I think what Paul is trying to do in this early section of Ephesians is to say "you have a really basic day to day life, it's called discipleship, it's called being faithful, it's called loving one another and what I want you to do is realize that that little life is now being thrust into the gargantuan narrative of God and what He has been doing in the cosmos from time eternal." It's as if our little story is thrust up into God's story so that our story has a deeper significance to it. When you've been most energized in your life is when whatever you are doing is connected with someone else, and then, someone else and still yet someone else. You can see your little acts have repercussions that go well beyond what you've just done. That's what Paul is trying to instill in the Christian community, the thought that one's little daily faithfulness is a major part of what God is doing in the world and in the cosmos itself.

The second observation I want to make concerns the prayer Paul offers after giving thanks for the people. In it he offers this petition: On a daily basis, I pray to God that He will give you wisdom and revelation. I like how N.T Wright translates the word "revelation"- "the ability to see things that most people don't see" (p. 392). "I pray that God will give you wisdom and the ability to see what most people won't see so that you might know Jesus." And here again, our English translators have done a less than adequate job. In Greek, the word "to know" is *ginosko*. But Paul uses an intensive of *ginosko*, *epiginosko*. The Jerusalem Bible says it best- "We are given wisdom and the ability to see that which most people can't see so that we might fully know the depths of Christ" (p. 331)

This is a knowledge that is deep and profound, but is not an end unto itself, because Paul says "I want you to use this knowledge so that the eyes of your heart will see who your hope is." You see, in Paul's day, just as in ours, there were a variety of people vying to offer us a place where our hope can reside. Paul wants to make sure we place hope in the right person. It reminds me of an observation that has been attributed to many, including Thomas Merton, "we climb the ladder of life giving our best effort, our money, and our time only to reach the top of the ladder and realize our ladder is leaning against the wrong wall." Paul wants to make sure that our life is leaning against the right wall. The hope of our life is a life leaning towards Christ. He is the one who will fulfill our life, so that at the end of life, we look out and we can see that we were leaning against the right wall.

The final observation I'm going to make is one that I think is the most difficult for us to really hear as modern people. It is connected to what was shared in the children's sermon, namely, the image that we, the church, are the body of Christ in the world. Paul states it this way: "It is through God's great power he raised Jesus from the dead and has made him Lord over all the universe, in fact He is now head of the Church; the Church which is the body of Christ which is filled with the fullness of the one who fills all things" (Ephesians 1:23).

I think most of us have heard that we, the church, are the body of Christ. We just haven't agreed to truly believe it. We read in the newspapers that churches do bad things; they continue to do bad things – evil things. And if you're a historian, there are all sorts of points in history where the Church has acted more like a tyrant than the Church. And so our modern minds, in an attempt to try and reconcile those facts, have basically placed the Church off to the side. A case in point being, that I was raised as a child in a tradition that almost saw the Church as the enemy - their concept of a community of faith was anti-church. We have a few folks in our neighborhood who advertise that way, "Come to us, we're not like a church." They realize that for many of us, church has a negative connotation.

I'm going to try to rediscover this truth from Paul by taking the text fairly literally. The Church IS the body of Christ filled with the fullness of Jesus. What has gone wrong, is not that the Church should be ignored; what has gone wrong is that the Church has misunderstood its commission.

The Church is the body of Christ; but what may I ask did Christ's body do? It showed up; it touched the untouchables; it healed those who were sick; it died. It gave itself up for humanity, in fact, for the world. If the Church is the body of Christ, maybe it needs to find its commission in being the kind of body that was lived out in Jesus. Namely that it be a gathering of people who offer themselves by showing up for others, touching those who are untouchable, offering healing to those who are sick and giving itself up, instead of a preservation of its existence.

And so I think this call to be the body of Christ in the world is one that we need to take seriously and it is one that we need to realize must be enfleshed: it can't just be a concept in our imagination. This image of the church being the body of Christ reminded me of one of my favorite quotes from Stanley Hauerwas and William Willimon in *Resident Aliens* where they say, "The church knows that its most credible form of witness and the most effective thing it can do for the world is the actual creation of a living, breathing, visible community of faith" (p. 47). In other words, what they're saying is we're called to be the living body of Christ in the world, not in theory but in actuality. Can we be the kind of community that enfleshes that which Jesus enfleshed? Can we be the kind of community that embodies the kind of self-giving, serving model of Jesus? Remember, Christ had God's power, and how did he use it? By serving others. That's the kind of body we're called to be. It's got to become a reality; it's got to become enfleshed, it can't just be talked about.

Now we come to the end of the sermon in which I promised you I would give you a practical application for you to go home with. This is very difficult step for me; I'm a theorist, I love theory; I just wish you all could take my theory and go out of here and figure it out yourself. But during this series, I am going to try my best to offer you some concrete examples. So how might we concretely be the Church that is the body of Christ in the world that lives its life out as Jesus lived?

I think that one of the things that allows us to be the Church, if we just took it seriously enough, is weekly worship. In other words if you're showing up and you are practicing what a radical community is supposed to look like, it might look like our weekly liturgy. The word "liturgy" simply means the work of the people. So every Sunday, I'm putting you to work practicing an alternative way of being community.

The ways of being a community are disguised in a bulletin, but it's there. We began this morning with a word of praise; we came and praised God as if God really mattered in a world that really wonders whether God ever shows up. And we began with praise in a world that seems to be far more concerned with destroying one another and complaining. We then moved to a time of confession in which we have the audacity to say, "I messed up," in a world that says, "I haven't messed up...you've messed up." And I wish our leaders could model something along those lines, but they often do more finger-pointing than confessing. So this is radical stuff-to show up and actually admit that we are at fault, that we have done something wrong, that we are broken. Then we have the audacity to actually listen to an ancient document, thousands of years old, and believe that it ought to have an authority in our life, that God actually speaks through it. This is odd because we live in a world where no one can tell me what to do, what to believe, or what to say. I am my own authority, thank you. In a few minutes we are going to offer our tithes and offerings; we are going to return a portion of what we believe God has entrusted to us as good stewards back to God's work. We live in a world that says, "it's my money, I'll give it if I feel like it, and you need to prove to me you deserve something from my bank account." And then a little after that, we're going to gather around the table and I'm going to say words like "everyone is welcome." Such profound truth is proclaimed in the midst of a world that seems to be far more concerned about who's not welcome, about building walls rather than bridges, about separating people into good and bad.

My friends, if we take this liturgy seriously, it's calling us to be the body of Christ in the world. Now these are tough actions to live out; that's why I said on Sunday we get to practice these things. But our hope is that after practicing it, we actually get to live it out in the world both as individuals and as a collective body.

I think this passage of scripture has much to share with us. We serve a God who is doing something that is far greater than what we can do alone. What we do is merged into what God is doing and so we are part of a much larger narrative. We are a people whom God is using to be the body of Christ in the world. It's not easy. But as our sending reminds us, we do not go out in the world on our own strength. We go out with the strength of the one who raised Jesus from the dead and who continues to fill the Church with the presence of Christ; so that the Church might fill the world and live and demonstrate to the world a different way of being. Amen.

Chapter Sources

Hauerwas, Stanley and William Willimon. <u>Resident Aliens</u>. Nashville: Abingdon Press, 1989.

Peterson, Eugene. <u>The Message</u>. Colorado Springs, Colorado: NavPress, 2002.

Pleonasm. (1999) Merriam-Webster's Collegiate Dictionary (p. 894, 10th edition). Springfield, Massachusetts: Merriam-Webster Incorporated.

The Jerusalem Bible. Garden City, New York: Doubleday & Company, Inc., 1966.

Wright, N.T. <u>The Kingdom New Testament</u>. New York, New York: Harper One, 2011.

Chapter 3

The Gospel Narrative: From Death to Life

Introduction

Everyone loves a good story. But unfortunately, as modern people we often see stories as simple narratives created to entertain us. This sermon develops the idea that narrative or story is more than just a fanciful tale; it is a doorway to truth. The power of the gospel according to Paul is the story of Jesus, but, it is more than a story. It is a revelation of God's grand narrative of salvation. That narrative has many versions, however in this section of Paul's letter to the Ephesians he provides a basic outline that summarizes all we need to know about who we are and what God has done to rectify our story.

Scripture: Ephesians 2:1-10

"You were dead through the trespasses and sins in which you once lived, following the course of this world, following the ruler of the power of the air, the spirit that is now at work among those who are disobedient. All of us once lived among them in the passions of our flesh, following the desires of flesh and senses, and we were by nature children of wrath, like everyone else. But God, who is rich in mercy, out of the great love with which he loved us even when we were dead through our trespasses, made us alive together with Christ – by grace you have been saved – and raised us up with him and seated us with him in the heavenly places in Christ Jesus, so that in the ages to come he might show the immeasurable riches of his grace in kindness toward us in Christ Jesus. For by grace you have been saved through faith, and this is not your own doing; it is the gift of God – not the result of works, so that no one can boast. For we are what he has made us, created in Christ Jesus for good works, which God prepared beforehand to be our way of life" (Ephesians 2:1-10, NRSV).

Sermon

One of the things that modernity has taught us well is that stories are not all that important. Stories are just fanciful tales that we make up to entertain ourselves. What's really important in life are the facts because the facts lead us to eternal principles, and our faith needs to be based upon those eternal principles and truths.

I find this line of thinking a little shocking because the bible that I read never really invites me to that way of understanding. The bible doesn't invite me to discover the hidden eternal truths via the facts of life, but rather, the bible seems to encourage me to become part of a narrative; to join the story of God and what God has done in the past, and what God continues to do in the present, and what God is going to do in the future. And this story, this narrative, is not something to entertain us; it is a story that helps define all of reality, how we live our lives and how we understand our lives. In the end it is a narrative that we must jump into.

There is nothing that I can prove about God's narrative from a scientific point of view; it's just a story. But I believe it's the story that makes all the difference in the world.

A good example of this is found in the opening lines of Paul's letter to the church at Ephesus in chapter 2. Paul draws a very bleak picture about his readers; they are dead in their sins, they are slaves to the powers of the universe, and they are children of wrath. One commentator has said that he doubts anyone in Ephesus would wake up in the morning thinking these things about themselves. The only way they could understand Paul's words is if they too, had leapt into the narrative of the gospel and understood that the gospel is trying to share a truth about them (and of course about us) in this world. That thought gave me a great opportunity (and excuse) to share another Hauerwas quote to you.

Stanley Hauerwas' book, *After Christendom*, includes a chapter I've always liked. One thing about Stanley is that most of the time you struggle to understand half of what he writes: but just read his chapter titles, they are really worth everything. Listen to this one, a chapter titled: "Why there is no salvation outside the church." (I just love that title…it grabs you. It's like, 'what's he going to say?'). One sentence in that chapter specifically applies to our sermon today. He says, "Without the church the world literally has no hope of salvation since the church is necessary for the world to know it is part of a story that it cannot know without the church" (p. 36).

In other words, Hauerwas is making the point that most people don't wake up in the morning saying "I need to be saved. I am just a wretched sinner in need of God's grace." The only way they know they are sinners in need of salvation is by hearing the gospel, by hearing the narrative that the church has been given, this is our story – it is everyone's story. I believe that Paul, whether he did this on purpose or not, outlines in these brief ten verses' three basic movements that describe what our "gospel" narrative is.

So, this morning I want to go through each one of these movements and help you to be convinced that you, too, ought to become a part of God's gospel narrative- from death to life.

In the first movement of the gospel Paul makes a statement about our human condition and it's a very bleak statement, but it is a very truthful statement from the perspective of the gospel. We are a people in dire need of being saved. Paul understands that most people don't really like to hear that. "You may need to be saved, but I don't need to be saved; I'm doing quite fine, thank you." And so he uses a little tactic here that he most likely learned from the prophet Amos.

Now, you probably haven't read Amos lately, so I will review it a little bit: Amos does this amazing thing at the beginning of his prophecy. He begins his message by condemning all the surrounding nations and enemies of Judah. He starts by condemning those in the south, and then he condemns those in the east, and then he condemns those to the north. He doesn't condemn anybody to the west because that's ocean. So, he gets around to three quarters, and you can almost hear voices in the background-- as you're reading Amos--people saying "Keep coming, keep coming: Yes, yes, keep it coming, brother"--and he ends his sermon by saying, "Oh and you, Judah, you are in a whole heap o' trouble…" And the Amens cease.

Paul does the same thing in a very subtle way- he begins by saying, "You…you were dead in your sins." If you remember Chapter 1, when Paul uses "you" he is tending to speak to the Gentile Christians in the church. When he uses the pronoun "we" he is tending to speak to the Jewish Christians in the church.

Paul was very aware of the tension between Jewish Christians and Gentile Christians, and so I imagine in a way he must have been thinking, "I'll start out with the Gentile Christians and get the Jewish Christians saying, 'Amen Brother Paul, that's exactly right; those Gentile Christians, they're in a whole heap of trouble'." But then in verse 3, he says suddenly, "Oh but all of us, we're all in the same boat, we're all children of wrath." In other words, in this first movement of the gospel, Paul says something that is very difficult for us to handle. He's telling us that we need to get on the same boat as those we see as "others". That's where forgiveness starts.

When we hear this first movement, there is a hesitancy to agree and say, "oh yeah, I'm on the same boat." If you doubt that, just look at the teachings of Jesus. He confronted Pharisees, who had the same hesitancy, and he said, "Why do you see the speck in your neighbor's eye, but do not notice the log in your own eye" (Matthew 7:3)? You see, it's so much easier to point the finger at somebody else. But like Amos, like Paul, like Jesus, the gospel begins with this simple statement; it's not to make us feel guilty, it's not to make us bummed out, it's just a statement: We are helpless in our condition of sin, and that, of course, leads to the second movement.

Many of you may not like the word "but" however this 'but' is a really good "but": "BUT God, who is rich in mercy, let me say that again, "God, who is rich in mercy, who has loved us even when we were dead in our sins, has given us life in Christ Jesus" (2:4).

This brief sentence defines the second movement. The very center of the gospel is the fact that our dire circumstances are remedied by God. And in this central movement, Paul affirms two things about God that I think we should never forget. The first is that God is rich in mercy. Many of you like God when he is rich in wrath for all those other people that need it. But Paul says God is rich in mercy, not rich in wrath. God is rich in mercy and I guarantee that this is not just the New Testament God, this is the God that was present from the very beginning. As Willimon says, "God's mercy is never based upon the circumstances of the world; God's mercy is based upon the character of God."

God has always been rich in mercy. And God who is rich in mercy *acts*- that's the second affirmation. God does something about those who are dead in their sins. God is the one who saves. I'm sure all of us know that in our heads. But listen to the way we talk sometimes about our faith: how I'VE accepted Jesus, or I'VE found God. You know--it suddenly becomes about ME...What I'VE done...Where I'VE been...and this text reminds us that the good news of the gospel starts only with God and not with me.

God in his rich mercy has given us new life. Paul says He has saved us. The Greek verb here, *sozo* is in the perfect tense and sometimes cannot be translated adequately in English. The perfect tense in Greek means that an act which has been completed in the past has ramifications for the present moment. God has saved us, and God continues to save us in the present moment. It's an action of God that takes a lifetime to complete and that of course leads us into the third movement.

We were helpless dead in our sins: but God who is rich in mercy has forgiven us, has continued to save us and now moves us into action. We are to become God's workmanship, not to somehow earn God's grace, because that grace came to us before we ever did anything for God. Because of what God has done, we now become the people that God has intended us to be, the workmanship of God.

So, what is the basis of that workmanship? The basis is what God did for us--namely that He was and is merciful. What we are called to do is to be people of mercy. Easier said than done. Another parable of Jesus: There once was a slave who owed his master great amounts of money. And one day he came before his master and his master said "Your debt is clear. You owe no more". The first thing the servant did upon receiving such an unbelievable act of grace was to approach another slave who owed him just a small amount of money. He said, "I need my money now," and when his brother said, "I don't have it," the first slave tossed the other into jail. Jesus says, "this guy just did not get it."

For me, this is the grand invitation of the gospel. Its narrative begins with my helplessness, its announcement is God's grace and mercy. Its invitation and challenge is to live as a people who show mercy, just as we have been forgiven.

This particular challenge goes right back to the beginning, where we find that it's so much easier to be forgiven than to forgive. It's so much easier to have God forgive me because, you know, I half-way deserve it, than to forgive you, who I may really question as being deserving of such an act. Do you see the dynamic here? The gospel invites us to live a life of mercy.

I came across a statement by Willimon about mercy that I thought was compelling. He goes back to the struggles that the early church had with the Roman Empire and finds that mercy was the one concept that Romans just could not get. He writes, "Mercy was the revolutionary defiant act that Jesus hurled in the face of the empire. Mercy was a main attraction as well as a chief repulsion in the evangelism of the Roman Empire. It was Christian mercy that made Christian minority a real threat. Mercy was the one Christian practice that baffled most imperial observers of the faith who knew that there were no classical intellectual means of explanation for such curious behavior. Fitful pagan provisions for the sick and the infirm were insignificant when compared with the veritable explosion of unprecedented Christian charity. Even the Emperor Julian, for all his animosity toward the faith. acknowledged, 'It is the Christians' philanthropy toward strangers, the care they take of the graves of the dead, and the affected sanctity with which they conduct the sanctity of their lives that has done the most to spread their atheism,' because he didn't believe they believed in God." Willimon concludes, in short, "Mercy was for Imperial Romans the strangest, the most countercultural of Christian practices. A virtue for which the entire classical, philosophical tradition provided them no help in comprehending" (Willimon, p. 52).

When the Church was the Church, it was merciful, and the world did not know how to respond to that. Of course, we inherit 1600 years of Christendom; the world is not all that surprised that Christians ought to be merciful. I guarantee you when we actually are, they still scratch their heads and think "Wow, I am utterly surprised."

So, your application this Sunday is go out and be merciful. How merciful? As merciful as God has been to you. For we are all on the same boat; it is called the boat of grace and forgiveness and mercy. And when we proclaim and live out that message, the world scratches its head and says: "Wow, what a strange group of people. Maybe, I should find out more about these folks."

Chapter Sources

Hauerwas, Stanley. <u>After Christendom</u>. Nashville: Abingdon Press, 1991.

Hauerwas, Stanley and William Willimon. <u>Resident Aliens</u>. Nashville: Abingdon Press, 1989.

Willimon, William. <u>Pulpit Resource Year B</u>- January, February, March 2012. Inver Grove Heights, MN: Logos Productions Inc.

Chapter 4

Remember When...But Now

Introduction

One of the first realities I had to adjust to when living in the Midwest was the lack of fences to divide residential properties. Having been raised in California, I was used to a good size fence in everyone's backyard. Fences allowed everyone to know the difference between my property and my neighbor's land.

A common variation on this theme is the prevalence of gated communities. Structures such as fenced yards and gated communities demarcate boundaries and, if properly used, can limit conflicts.

The text for this sermon uses the imagery of a wall as a physical sign of a profound division among people. It proclaims that Jesus came to break down this wall and to create in our midst a new reality. It is the hope of this sermon that the listener will reflect on their own experiences with walls, fences or any barrier that seeks to divide, allowing the words of Paul to offer a contrasting reality.

Scripture: Ephesians 2:11-22

"So then, remember that at one time you Gentiles by birth, called 'the uncircumcision' by those who are called 'the circumcision' – a physical circumcision made in the flesh by human hands – remember that you were at that time without Christ, being aliens from the commonwealth of Israel, and strangers to the covenants of promise, having no hope and without God in the world. But now in Christ Jesus you who once were far off have been brought near by the blood of Christ. For he is our peace; in his flesh he has made both groups into one and has broken down the dividing wall, that is, the hostility between us. He has abolished the law with its commandments and ordinances, that he might create in himself one new humanity in place of the two, thus making peace, and might reconcile both groups to God in one body through the cross, thus putting to death that hostility through it. So he came and proclaimed peace to you who were far off and peace to those who were near; for through him both of us have access in one Spirit to the Father. So then you are no longer strangers and aliens, but you are citizens with the saints and also members of the household of God, built upon the foundation of the apostles and prophets, with Christ Jesus himself as the cornerstone. In him the whole structure is joined together and grows into a holy temple in the Lord; in whom you also are built together spiritually into a dwelling place for God" (Ephesians 2:11-22, NRSV).

Sermon

This passage of scripture is very evocative. Some of the images are a bit negative--that we are people without God; some are quite positive--that we are a new humanity created in Christ; some can be quite hopeful--that we are the temple of God. But for me, in my own walk, the most powerful image is that of the dividing wall.

In 2010 my wife and I had the opportunity to tour the holy land for about 10 days. I had read about the wall that divides Israel from Palestine, but it wasn't until I saw it, and actually drove next to it, that I realized that this 35-foot cement barrier had a way of affecting me physically, and it wasn't a positive impression. Now, in my head I knew why this wall had been built and some of the reasons for its construction even made sense. But to actually be there, to actually drive next to this wall, it just reminded me of the deep division that walls are associated with. It is this depth of division that I think Paul wants us to take into our interpretation of this passage as he begins to address what Christ has done to those walls that so easily divide us.

But, of course, I'm getting ahead of myself-- that's point number 2 in this sermon. Actually this week's sermon is a fairly easy one to grasp in that Paul almost echoes the three movements we discussed last Sunday (2:1-10). Movement one is a description of our human situation and it's never very positive. Movement two is what God, or Christ, has done to address the human condition, and movement three is what we do (or should do) in response to what Christ has done. The same movements that were present in 1-10 are present here in 11-22. So I think we want to go through these three, acknowledging that the movements are much the same, but also being aware that the content and the focus are a bit different.

In movement one in this week's text, when Paul talks about our condition, he concentrates mostly on Gentile Christians and he sees their situation through the eyes of Israel. He says you (gentiles) are the uncircumcised and "without Christ." I think that is an unfortunate translation. *Christos* in Greek can be translated "Christ" or "Messiah" and we tend to associate Messiah with the people of Israel. So, without Messiah, gentiles are not a part of the commonwealth of Israel and thus are strangers to the covenants. They are without hope; they are *atheos*. We could translate that word as "atheist," but it would be better to simply say, "Without God," because our concept of atheist is a person who doesn't believe in God. There would not be a person in the first century who didn't believe in some god. There were no modern-day atheists in Paul's day. So, what Paul is talking about here can be more accurately stated by the phrase "you gentiles were apart from the God who are called the people of Israel and made the covenant and established this commonwealth- you were, to put it mildly, God forsaken. You were afar." This situation is quite dire as far as Paul is concerned, and this sets up the movement into the second phase of his argument.

So, in verse 13 we get--and the Greek is really pretty clear--*nuni de*, (whenever you see *nuni de* you know there's a transition going on), which is translated "but now" in English (doesn't sound as good as *nuni de*, does it?). *Nuni de*, "but now, in Christ, you who were far off have been brought near" (Ephesians 2:13)

I think before we move on to discuss the great imagery here, we need to highlight that the verb "to bring" is expressed in the passive voice. In other words, the Gentiles didn't decide to come to God, they were brought by Christ to God. They didn't decide for themselves; a decision was made for them. The gentiles were brought to God through Christ and what Christ did--which was abolishment of the dividing wall that had separated gentiles and the Jewish people for centuries.

When you break down the Greek words for "dividing" and "wall" they're fairly neutral and innocuous. The word for "dividing" simply means "a wall that separates interior rooms inside a house." And the word for "wall" is better translated as "a fence." A fence that doesn't actually separate, but a fence that simply protects. But somehow, when you put these two Greek words together, what you get is a very foreboding image of a deep, dark division between Jews and Gentiles. If we were to use modern day imagery, we would say something like the

"Iron curtain" or the "Berlin Wall." If we want to apply it sociologically, we would say (especially those of you who were raised in the '40's and '50's), "they were born on the wrong side of the tracks," or, "...we're going through a bad neighborhood, please lock the doors."

You know those walls, right? Those walls that separate people; separate societies...some of them are physical, some of them are not...that's what Paul is talking about. You see, most scholars believe that his frame of reference for the wall was the 5-foot wall that appeared in the temple, and on it was a plaque that said "If you are not a Jew, and you go past this barrier, you are susceptible to capital punishment [to death]." It was the barrier that kept the temple for the Jews and only the Jews. And Paul says that barrier has now been crushed, even though it had been built upon a foundation of God's laws and ordinances.

I want us to pause here, because I think sometimes, we miss the positive aspect. The original intent of the laws and ordinances was not to draw a division between people, it was to help the people of Israel be more faithful. When you read the Old Testament accounts there's joy in receiving the law. The law describes how they ought to be as a people. It gives them some distinct activities to do, but nowhere does it cause, at least in the original text, a division.

But what happened is that the people took what was supposed to enhance their spiritual walk and their faithfulness and made it into a separation, so that they saw themselves as holy and everyone else as unholy. They saw themselves as faithful, and everyone else as condemned.

Some of you may remember the story I've told about my experience with the Navigators when I was in college. The

Navigators are a group of very intense disciples of Christ who offer tools to enhance your spiritual walk. The Navigators' intent is to help you grow as a Christian. Unfortunately, after two years of being a Navigator on a Christian campus, I began to see the group as creating a dividing wall, because the people I hung around with saw the Navigator's tools as clear signs that this group believed they were spiritually superior to 99% of the people on campus. We Navigators walked around believing that we were closer to God because of all of the things we did that we knew the other students on campus weren't doing. What was intended to enhance our spiritual walk, we used as a barrier, in effect saying, "We're in; you're out. We're near; you're far." And so Paul says--in the second movement--that when Christ comes, He comes to break all that down; to obliterate distinctions, to create within us a new humanity. In Christ's world, those distinctions are no longer important.

Just as during last week's sermon, this seems like a pretty good place to stop...does that sound good? But Paul wants to go further, because Paul never allows the good news to just end with an affirmation. He wants to say, "Well, what does that mean in my life?" So in verse 19 he says, so now you are no longer the old "you." (Remember at the beginning of the text he says you need to remember what you were.) And now he says that "you" are no longer, and he uses different kinds of images to make the point: an image of relationship - you're no longer a stranger, a social image - you're no longer an alien, you are part of God's family. In fact, you are the temple in which God's Spirit dwells.

In light of what Christ has done for the world, Paul says we are to be a community, not just individuals. We are to be a people who embody what Christ embodied, which was a presence that, upon finding walls, breaks them down rather than builds

44

them up. Because the text is very clear that when Jesus broke down the walls, it came at a great cost. The text says in his own body Jesus bore this division. This is a gentle reminder. Too often I think that in our minds, when we think of Jesus dying on the cross, that we see him dying just to deal with our sin. Paul loves to stretch that out; the cross for him is so fundamental, it can't be limited to the forgiveness of sins. For Paul, Jesus died on the cross so that we may have a relationship with God and one another. He reconciles us to God and to one another. He breaks down the divisions that are so quickly erected among us.

I wish that I could end the sermon with that third movement and say, "Praise be to God, we're doing it; I have no illustrations to the contrary." But unfortunately, we're not doing it very well.

A survey was taken of Christians by LifeWay Research in which the respondents were simply asked this question: "Do you prefer to worship with people of the same political slant as you?" 47% of the participants said, "Yes, that would be my desire"; 42% said "no" and 11% are still trying to decide. So, there's not a majority, but I don't know…47% is way too high for my tolerance level. It's almost as if we're moving into a place where on our banner we need to say "Welcome to Shepherd of the Sierra," then put our political affiliation and clearly state that only you who are (fill in the blank) are welcome, because the majority of our folks don't want to worship with any of the other folks.

I call that "wall creating," "wall building." And I just read that Jesus gave his life to what? To do just the opposite-- tear down walls. I wish I could say it was easy, but it's not. I'm going to end with a positive illustration, at least I think it's a positive one, someone who I think at least got the message right. When

I first read this, I remembered the story, but I never really knew the story behind the story. This story is about something that happened back in May of 2009 - some of you may remember this. Then President Barack Obama was to be given an honorary doctorate at the University of Notre Dame, and it caused all sorts of controversy on campus amongst many faculty and students. Why? Because he was pro-choice, and the Catholic Church is pro-life on the issue of abortion. And so their thinking was why would we give an honorary doctorate to someone who voluntarily violates church rules and the position of the church?

So it was very controversial. Yet it was still decided by the University that Obama would get his Honorary degree. What the President of Notre Dame said is most important for all of us to hear today. Addressing the students in his introduction of President Obama, Father John Jenkins, President of Notre Dame, described the situation in which we live in this way: "The world you enter into today is torn by division and is fixed on its differences. Differences must be acknowledged and, in some cases, cherished...but too often, differences lead to pride in one's self or in one's little tribe and contempt for others. Too often differences lead to hostility and enmity; too often differences end up with two sides taking opposing views of the same difference and demonizing each other, whether the difference is political, religious, racial, or national, trust fails, anger rises, and cooperation ends even for the sake of causes all sides care about. More than any problem in the arts or sciences, easing the hateful divisions between human beings is the supreme challenge of this age. If we can solve this problem, we have a chance to come together and solve all the others." (as cited in Verhey and Harvard, pp. 106-107)

There are some great truths in his words, and I think it is quite reflective of what Paul is trying to say Jesus is about. So I know my words are not going to change the world. I know I am going to stand before you next week and have all sorts of reasons to share with you why the world is falling apart. Our message for application this day is that we need to go from this place and begin to practice the ministry that Christ practiced on the cross; where we see walls, where we see divisions, we break them down, we reach across, we make connection. We don't demonize those who disagree with us; we become the body of Christ that is the dwelling place of God's Spirit. Do you think God's Spirit wants to dwell with no one other than Republicans or Democrats??? You've got to be kidding. Now those of you who are Independent, you may vote for that – but it's utterly ridiculous! God's Spirit dwells with God's people. What identifies us is not our party affiliation or our political point of view, but our baptism. Our baptism is by one who gave his life to break down walls so our job is to break down walls as well, and to be that reconciling community that makes a difference in the world, one person at a time. Amen.

Chapter Sources

christianitytoday.com/news/2018/August

Verhey, Allen and Joseph S. Harvard. <u>Ephesians</u> (Belief Commentary). Louisville, KY: Westminster/John Knox Press, 2011

Chapter 5

Life as a Prayer to God

Introduction

When I was a child, I sang a song that many of us know, "Jesus Loves Me." It is a simple yet profound song. Jesus does love me, as well as you, as well as the whole world. This sermon seeks to address this simple, yet important, bottom line. The message of the gospel is about God's love for us and God's call for us to love others. It is a message that has been proclaimed throughout the ages, but yet, a message that begs repetition; for our human proclivity is to embrace God's love of me, and too easily forget my call to love others. This prayer of Paul's reminds us that when we are a people that live out God's love, that we truly are a people who are surrounded by God's love.

Scripture: Ephesians 3:14-21

"For this reason I bow my knees before the Father, from whom every family in heaven and on earth takes its name. I pray that, according to the riches of his glory, he may grant that you may be strengthened in your inner being with power through his Spirit, and that Christ may dwell in your hearts through faith, as you are being rooted and grounded in love. I pray that you may have the power to comprehend, with all the saints, what is the breadth and length and height and depth, and to know the love of Christ that surpasses knowledge, so that you may be filled with all the fullness of God. Now to him who by the power at work within us is able to accomplish abundantly far more than we can ask or imagine, to him be glory in the church and in Christ Jesus to all generations, forever and ever. Amen." (Ephesians 3:14-21, NRSV).

Sermon

I'm sure some of you have had the experience of talking about something, briefly diverging into another subject, and then forgetting what you were originally talking about. Many scholars believe this may have happened to Paul in the third chapter of the book of Ephesians. That's the premise, and if you want to pull out the bible, you can actually see there's some proof, or at least some evidence hinting of a divergence. Our text (starting with verse 14) begins with the words "For this reason," but if you look at your bible in verse 1 of chapter 3, you see the same words, "For this reason."

So here's the theory: Paul has just proclaimed the amazing news of the inclusion of Gentiles in God's plan. The dividing wall that separated Jew from Gentile has been completely obliterated by the body of Christ. Those who are far off have been brought near - this is fabulous news and Paul is excited by this news! The argument states that Paul wishes to move right into a time of prayer, but just as he states, "For this reason, I bow my knee", he thinks of something. Maybe he suddenly wonders if his readers will actually believe what he is stating, namely this amazing news about the inclusion of the Gentiles into the gospel story. Thus, verses 1-13 are a testimonial regarding Paul as to his calling and authority as an apostle of Jesus.

I'm not going to preach on these verses, simply because I've run out of Sundays between now and Advent to cover the whole book of Ephesians. So, let me just give you a brief summary of what Paul says in these verses. He notes that some of the Ephesian Christians were once "far off" and now have been "brought near." This new reality is very much like Paul's own story. In effect he's saying "even though you are Gentiles and I'm a Jew, I was far off because I was persecuting the church. Then the risen Christ came to me in a vision and brought me near and gave me this calling to share the good news with all Gentiles, that they are a part of God's plan of salvation. And then he catches himself and says, "Oh yeah, for this reason," and he then returns to the prayer he had started a few verses before. Now this explanation for the seemingly repetition of this phrase "for this reason" in both verse 1 and verse 14 is only a theory; I found it a creative one, because it makes Paul very human: going one way, and getting distracted, then coming back to where he needed to be in the first place.

In today's text Paul does come back to this need for a prayer, and he begins this prayer by praying to "the Father from whom all families in heaven and earth receive their name." Paul is using a little play on words that you can only see in the Greek. The word for "father" in Greek is *pater*, the word for "family" is *patria*, and so you see the connection between God the Father and the families. There is, in fact a deep connection; God is the one who has created all the families, all the people.

Paul is talking about the same reflection of reality that was shared in Chapter 2: if God has included the Gentiles in His plan for salvation, then God is the God of all creation; all God's people are His children. I like what Steven Fowl says in his commentary--that this verse establishes who God truly is. As Fowl puts it, "this is no tribal deity, no local God, not just the God of our ancestors. This God is not just committed to a flourishing of a particular culture, country or family; this God is the God of all the families of the earth -- the God of all things" (p. 124)

I think this is an important starting point for this prayer – Paul offers a prayer to the God of all people. Now, we know that God is the creator of all people. We know this, but really don't know this. Have you ever had days in which you begin believing that God's children include all the people on the earth? Then, in the midst of driving down the road someone cuts you off and you conclude that particular person couldn't have been God's creation to do something like that. Or someone disagrees with you, or you have someone who's been a lifelong enemy--what was God thinking when He created him or her? There must have been another God who created that person.

Or, maybe this captures your reality, someone disagrees with you and you have that sense that God is on your side and every argument the other person is giving must be demonic in some way. We play these games in an attempt to try to raise those dividing walls that separate us. But Paul will have nothing to do with that; he says I pray to the God, our Father, from whom all families, all people, all tribes, all nations, all communities have been given names by the same God. In these words of Paul, you can hear the echoes of Genesis, as God names all of creation.

This is an important starting point; it's one I think we always need to remember. That the God we serve can never be a tribal, nationalistic God, or a God of a particular racial group. God is God of ALL people everywhere, at all times, in all places, even those places where others may be giving us trouble.

Once God's eminence has been established, Paul then offers three petitions: these petitions are hard to decipher in the English, because Paul is typical Paul; he just loads on phrase after phrase after phrase. From verses 16-19 there is one gargantuan Greek sentence that makes very little sense, except for some markers in the Greek text that allow you to see where Paul is actually pausing and breathing. He uses a little word called *hina* and it appears three times. With each *hina*, I can assume he is offering a separate petition because one of the functions of *hina* is to demark a particular line of thinking.

The first petition is a very long one. It starts with verse 16. Paul prays and his prayer is for the church. This is something we need to remember; all of the pronouns here are plural. So this is not a prayer for individuals, but for the entire church; it's a prayer for the community of faith. He prays that the church would gain strength in their inner being through the power of the Spirit, as the people allow Christ to dwell in their midst, as they are rooted and grounded in love. This is very wordy, but it's almost like the layers are connected to each other, so you could start at the beginning, or at the end.

We are called to the community of faith to be strengthened through the Holy Spirit by keeping Christ at the center of our ministry--and Christ only dwells in communities that are grounded and rooted in love. Or, alternatively, we've got to begin with the grounding and rooting of love, then Christ will dwell there, and when Christ dwells, the Spirit gives us power. It works either way, but they are all connected.

What I consider to be really important for us to understand is that often times when we think of the church (and I think it's one of the reasons we individualize prayer), we tend to think of a building, an institution, a set of programs that entice us, a dynamic worship service, a place to go on Sunday. But Paul pictures the church as all of you – us. We are the church and this church's foundation is built on one thing and that is love. Because it is love that allows Christ to dwell and when Christ dwells, the Spirit gives us power.

This is something that I have shared with you over and over again: the bottom line for the church is not a nice building, an effective staff, a balanced ledger sheet, or even a dynamic worship service. The bottom line of the church is love. If we don't get that right, we're fooling ourselves. Paul says the same thing in another way in another book: "If I speak with human eloquence and angelic ecstasy, but don't love, I'm nothing but the creaking of a rusty gate. If I speak God's words with power, revealing all His mysteries, making everything as plain as day and if I have faith that says to a mountain, jump, and it jumps but I don't love, I am nothing. If I give everything I own to the poor and even go to the stake to be burned as a martyr, but I don't love, I have gotten nowhere. So, no matter what I say, what I believe and what I do I'm bankrupt without love" (1 Corinthians 13:1-3, The Message). That, my friends, is Paul's bottom line. I think it ought to be our bottom line as well. We can't get out of the gate unless we learn this love thing. And to help you out, that's all I'm going to talk about the rest of the day, because I think that this is what this prayer is all about, getting the love thing right.

The second petition seems to connect with the previous petition in a tangential way, and yet I think it is fundamental to Paul's thought. The second petition has to do with mystery. Paul says, "I desire that you be able to comprehend the love of Christ" and then, at the end of the petition, he says that such love "surpasses human knowledge." In other words, you'll know that which can't be known. Now, some people call that an oxymoron: "I pray that you will comprehend that which is incomprehensible. I pray that you will know that which you can't know." The mystics have a great awareness of this reality, it's called embracing the mystery, walking into the mystery, being a part of the mystery, not having the certitudes of knowing everything, just simply walking in and knowing that the love of Christ surrounds you and holds you.

Those of you who have read Richard Rohr may recognize this particular quote. Rohr says: "Enlightenment is not as much about knowing as it is about unknowing. It is not so much learning, as unlearning; it is about surrendering and letting go rather than achieving and possessing. It is more about entering the mystery than arriving at a mental certitude. Enlightenment is all gratuitous grace, and the only reasonable response is a grateful heart and the acknowledgement that always there is more to the mystery" (p. 38). Paul prays that the community of faith will be a community that walks in the mystery of Christ's love; a love that is so incomprehensible there's no way we can know it all. We are surrounded by this love and we walk in it.

Another way of translating the word "comprehend" is "to grasp." I am going to play with Paul a little bit here. He prays that we would grasp the love of Christ. So as we walk through the mystery, we don't grasp certitude, or the facts, or the truth, or that I'm right, and you're wrong. We simply walk in the mystery and we grasp--what? The love of Christ. We grasp on to the Love of Christ. That allows us to walk in a world that I believe needs to understand that it's far more mysterious than it is known.

This leads to the final petition which comes at the end of verse 19. I like the way the New English Bible translates it: "May you obtain the fullness of being; the fullness of God himself." Paul's prayer is that we, the church, would be filled with the fullness of God. My question to you is, if we are filled with ourselves and our own certitude, where does God fit? On the sidelines, agreeing with us? If we let go of those certitudes, if we let go of those things that we think are most important, we empty ourselves, and then what do we get filled with but the fullness of God. And what is that fullness of God? It is God's love, the mystery of Christ, the love that is foundational to the life of the church. It all comes back to this--the fullness of God cannot be understood unless we love.

Have you ever noticed some people who want to cling to certitude and facts are not all that loving when they converse with others they disagree with? They use their certitude as a hammer and beat the other person up, whereas love welcomes the other. Here's another Rohrism: "Please hear this from the saints and the mystics: God never leads the soul through guilt, shame or fear but attracts the soul through love" (p. 199).

The fullness of God is achieved when we are a community that is filled with love. If we are a community that manipulates people, that blames people, that shames people, God's fullness cannot reside in us because that is not God's modus operandi, that's ours. We need to understand that this prayer is calling us forth to be a community, a community that is rooted and grounded in love; so that Christ may dwell in our midst, that the Spirit might empower us, so that we have the ability to grasp onto the love of Christ as we walk through the mysteries of this world. When we are that kind of community, we can be empty so that Christ's fullness can fill us, and we then can be a community that is truly a reflection of God's full being.

What does the bible say that God is? God is love--see I told you I was going to repeat this over and over again. I think it's an important message for us to hear. This is Paul's prayer for the church at Ephesus. I believe it is Paul's prayer for every church.

I said that during this series on Ephesians I would end the sermon with an application. And while I believe that this prayer is being prayed for the church, the church is made up of individuals. I would like us to think about our own individual spiritual walk and what this message might mean to us. I don't know what kind of week you've had. Maybe this week's been a really good week. Maybe it's not been a very good week, but I guarantee you that no matter whether it's been a good week or a bad week, coming to church and hearing that you are a creature of God and loved by your creator, and that you are to go out and love the world, is a message we all need to hear, right?

So that's where we're going to end, on the important note that the community of faith seeks to be filled with the fullness of God; and we then begin to understand that we are loved by our creator.

I came across a quote from a 14th century nun, Catherine of Siena, and I think the quote speaks of that desire. This is what she writes: "The love a soul sees that God has for her she in turn extends to all creatures. She sees how fully she herself is loved by God when she beholds herself in her source: the sea of God's being. She then desires to love herself in God and God in herself like a person, who on looking into the water sees his or her own image there and, in this vision, loves and delights in self" (Fowl, p. 121). It is a beautiful thought by a very dedicated and holy woman--that we would be a people filled with the fullness of God, walking through this sea of God's being, that is nothing but love, letting only this word, God's fullness, God's love for us, fill our hearts and help identify who we are in Christ. Amen.

Chapter Sources

Fowl, Stephen. Ephesians (The New Testament Library). Louisville, KY: Westminster/John Knox Press, 2012.

Peterson, Eugene. The Message. Colorado Springs, CO: Navpress, 2002.

Rohr, Richard. On the Threshold of Transformation. Chicago: Loyola Press, 2010

Chapter 6

Called to Community

Introduction

One of the distinctive aspects of Pauline theology centers in his proclivity to offer a theological foundation followed by an ethical call to practice what we believe. In chapter four of his letter to the church in Ephesus, Paul does just that with power and clarity, "I beg you to lead a life worthy of the calling to which you have been called." No clearer words can be found in scripture than here concerning this call to live out our faith.

This sermon seeks to not only recognize this shift, but to articulate the specific acts that Paul desires of his readers. These acts are centered in community life, an ongoing concern of this book and of our life in these days.

Scripture: Ephesians 4:1-6

"I therefore, the prisoner in the Lord, beg you to lead a life worthy of the calling to which you have been called, with all humility and gentleness, with patience, bearing with one another in love, making every effort to maintain the unity of the Spirit in the bond of peace. There is one body and one Spirit, just as you are called to the one hope of your calling, one Lord, one faith, one baptism, one God and Father of all, who is above all and through all and in all" (Ephesians 4:1-6, NRSV).

Sermon

I'm going to begin our time together by quoting Professor Richard Ward who is commenting about this passage of scripture in light of the time of year that this particular text appears in the lectionary.

This particular passage from Ephesians appears in the lectionary, around year B in the middle of July or August. And thus, the professor is making his comments based on the fact that this text is read in the deep months of summer. He says: "It is a shame that the lectionary appoints a text like this for ordinary time when it doesn't have the best chance of getting the hearing it deserves. Here is an extraordinary text that has startling relevance for congregations who are asking basic questions about Christian identity and purpose. To bypass this ancient text is to miss the opportunity it affords to address some vexing issues for ministry in this time and this place. The fractious church's need to hear grace notes and exhortations on the themes of unity and diversity is acute, as is its hunger for doxology, which is just a fancy way of saying 'praise', and direction. The human community is in desperate need of communities of faith where belief and practice are congruous" (Ward, p. 303)

I couldn't agree more. This particular set of scriptures offers some of the best that we're going to hear in all of Ephesians. I've engaged with Ephesians for many years and have always realized that, of course, as you read through chapters one, two and three there are some really good messages. But then you hit chapter four--wow! This is really a powerful message. Chapters four, five and six are some of the best material you're going to hear from Paul. I hope that you embrace this fabulous passage, it has a lot to say to us.

This passage begins with one little Greek word, *oun*, which means, "therefore." We all know, before you can have a "therefore" there needs to be a "wherefore." The "wherefore" is found in chapters one, two and three. Paul, has established the good news of the gospel (the "wherefore"). We hear it more as a message of praise and doxology than as some kind of taciturn lecture on doctrine. Paul is simply saying that, in Christ, everything has changed. The mysteries of God's plan for salvation have been revealed; the dividing wall that separated Jew from Gentile has been obliterated in the body of Christ. We are now being created as a new humanity. It is the church that is the context in which God's creation is occurring.

More precisely, Paul is establishing our identity, who we are. Christ has made us into something new and is continuing to make us into something new. And now he's saying, based on that reality, I want you to BE something. He says, "I want you to live a life worthy of the calling to which you've been called." This is the tough stuff -- we know what we are, now do it, now be it, now live it out--the rubber meeting the road.

This is what chapter four is all about--this is what makes chapters four, five and six so important. Paul begins to apply the theology of chapters one, two and three within the context of the real world. He begins this passage of scripture by urging or, as in our text read today, "begging" his readers to follow in this new way of being. The Greek word there is *parakelleo*; a word Paul uses pervasively in his writings. It can mean anything from "I direct you," or "I command you," or "I encourage you." I like the translation of "encouragement" far better than "beg" or even "command." I "encourage" you... but it's a strong encouragement.

Such strong encouragement reminds me of the people in my life who have meant the most to me. Now, I happen to be a "school geek," which meant I really was sad when I had to miss school. I loved school, and it shouldn't surprise you that some of the folks I remember most vividly in my life are teachers and professors who demanded, who encouraged, who commanded me to be a better student. I had professors who didn't give me the grades I thought I deserved because they knew there was something deeper in me, something better that needed to be called forth. When I was in seminary, I had the opportunity to actually teach my fellow students New Testament Greek and I was scared to death because I didn't know the language all that well. But I had a professor who said, "you stay a day ahead of them and you can do this." And I did! But he was also the one who never gave me an "A." Even so, Dr. Deasly was someone I'll always, always remember. That's what Paul's doing; he's calling forth this congregation in Ephesus to be who you are in Christ, to own your identity, to allow your identity to determine how you live, how you see the world, how you conduct yourself within the world.

I always liked the little story that William Willimon tells of himself. He said: "I can still remember the voice of my mom as I shut the door as I was leaving for a Friday night date. She would say, 'Will, remember you're a Willimon.'" And he continues, "I don't know if it really went all that deep when I was 16 or 17, but now as an adult, I realized what she was saying. When I went out on that date, she was calling me to remember the community, the family, that had shaped and formed me; that had given me values; that had given me a sense of who I was. Don't forget that; don't lay that aside; be who you are; allow your identity to dictate every action you take, even on a Friday night date" (Oral sharing by Dr. Willimon).

I think that is what Paul is telling us as a church--to be all that we can be in Christ. Christ has done something amazing, to the

61

extent that we do not need to try to change. Christ has already changed us.

In this text, Paul offers us two encouragements or urgings. The first one looks like four statements, but in actuality Paul offers three qualities followed by one urging. The qualities are humility, gentleness, and patience. The urging is "bear one another in love". What I think he's saying is I want you to bear one another in love. How you do that is by being humble, being gentle, and being patient.

I could go on for a long time with this passage. But we need to back away and make some basic observations about Paul's first encouragement. In these words, we observe something we all know, namely, that love can never be understood in the abstract. Love is not a concept; love is a relationship between two people; that's what makes it fun and difficult all at the same time. Marcus Barth, in his commentary states: "According to this passage, there is no love except in relation to specific neighbors. Love is not a disposition of the soul which can be perfect in itself without being given and shaped in ever new concrete encounters." And I love his concluding sentence, "It is always specific, always costly, always a miraculous event" (p. 428). Love is specific, love is costly, love in the end is a miracle... it's a miracle.

Paul says the church is a community of faith gathered in the name of Christ, and that community ought to "bear one another up in love." The kind of love he's talking about is not just a nice little smile and I love y'all comment. It's the kind of love where I am called to "bear you up." I've got to carry you. I don't know if Paul means, "you are a pain to me"--could be. Or it could be that Paul knows that to truly love another person, to walk alongside them costs something. It costs something from us. We can't be in relationship without it costing something. And we willingly bear that cost because we're in relationship, we're in love. Paul says that's the kind of community of faith we need to be; a community that is bound by carrying each other's burdens, especially when we are too weary to carry our own heavy load.

The qualities by which we do this, according to Paul, are qualities that his original readers would not have seen in a very positive light. These qualities are humility and gentleness. Most commentators observe that in the ancient Greek world, words such as humility and gentleness were not positive characteristics. So why does Paul use them? Because they were the characteristics of Jesus. In Philippians, Paul says that even though Jesus was God, he emptied himself and he became humble. He became a servant.

If you look at the life of Jesus, he is always gentle with people. Now it doesn't mean that he's not direct or to the point, but his overall manner is quite gentle. He sees people's stories. He sees the other as a real person, they're not just an issue. And he's also patient with people. My definition of patience, as Jesus demonstrates it, is that he allows space for people to make their own choice; he never twists arms, he never makes people feel guilty. He pretty much says, "This is what it's going to cost you, come follow me." And, He gives them space to decide. Remember the case of a young ruler who eventually says, "Whoa, that's too much of a cost for me, Jesus" and walks away? I've always speculated that the ruler eventually came back because he was almost there, Christ is patient, gentle, humble; that's the kind of community we need to be.

Paul's other urging concerns unity. "May you maintain the unity of the Spirit in the bond of peace." The key word here for me is "maintain." Paul could have said, you need *to create* unity; you need *to make up* unity; you need *to strive* for unity; you need to get a small group with unity; you need to have the objective of unity; you need to have a focus on unity – he could have said all of those. But he says, "maintain" unity. What Paul states is that the unity of the Spirit is already there. When a person is baptized, he or she is baptized into the community, the body of Christ; a unified body.

I wish I could stand before you and say, in the past 2000 years, Christians have maintained that unity well. But we haven't. We are a fractured people. I read a statistic recently that there are more than 35,000 denominations around the world. We have taken that which was one, which was a unified body and for all sorts of good reasons have divided it, right? When has a church ever split over bad reasons, right? If you are the splitter, there's always a good reason to go away from the splittee. But Paul says, "NO…the Church is ONE!"

We are to maintain unity, and the example he gives is our belief, our affirmation. Now, many people believe this statement of belief is a brief hymn that Paul has quoted, we really don't know. It definitely has a unique style. We observe that there are 7 "ones" in the hymn and 7, of course, is a biblical number for perfection. There are also three sets of triads, although the third triad begs a bit of creativity.

The first two triads are fairly easy, but if you look at all three you have the beginning outline of the trinity. Paul says, we have one body, one spirit, one hope – first triad points to God the Spirit; one Lord, one faith, one baptism; that's Jesus. We have one God, now here comes the more tricky triad: "who is above all, in all, and through all". Paul is proclaiming that our unity is a given. This unity can be stated by confessing that which we have in common. I am utterly convinced that most denominations would cease to exist if we really got around to counting the number of beliefs that we actually have in common, and then counting the number of things we disagree on. The agreements would far out-weigh the disagreements.

Of course we Presbyterians have majored in making those distinctions seem really important, as have other denominations. Again, I think if we lined it all up, we have far more in common than that which divides us, and yet we remain divided. I believe that Paul calls us to be a community of faith; a community that understands that the divisions we create may seem important at the time, but they are not ultimately what God desires of us. We are to be a people who are "to maintain the unity of the Spirit in the bond of peace" (Ephesians 4:3b, NRSV). It is a calling for us to be a people who understand that our one Lord is the reason we are one, not because we all can agree on the same doctrines.

I want to end this sermon by giving you a series of practices. So here are your practices: go out this week, start being humble. If you get that one down, move on to gentleness. You get that one accomplished, go on to patience. And when you get that one completed, move on to bearing one another in love. If you get that one realized, you can do the unity thing. I have a feeling most of us will probably be able to address the first and maybe the second of those practices, with only the hope we will get to 3, 4, or 5. But that's what the walk of faith is all about. It's about being a community that really cares about one another. We care for each other by being humble in each other's presence, by being gentle with each other, by being patient with each other, by bearing one another's burdens, by maintaining unity of Spirit in the bond of peace.

I came across a fabulous quote that I will use to end this sermon. It comes from Desmond Tutu's book, *No Future without Forgiveness*. Some of you may remember that after apartheid fell, and Nelson Mandela was freed from prison and subsequently elected President of South Africa, he developed a Truth and Reconciliation Commission headed by Bishop Tutu. It was Desmond Tutu's job to try to bring healing to a nation whose only memory was of persecution, warfare, bloodshed, and hatred. When you met someone from the other side of the conflict, you could actually picture the people in your family that that person had killed or imprisoned. In other words, there was a lot of basis to keep this cycle of hatred and animosity going. You can almost hear the skeptics sarcastically saying, "Oh Desmond, we know you wish to bring some reconciliation amidst our hurt, we know you would desire to bring both sides together and seek to bring some kind of truth that is spoken in reconciling love...but be real Desmond, it is not possible." It was a seemingly impossible task!

Here's where that word comes in and becomes pertinent. That word is *Ubuntu*. Bishop Tutu used it to describe what such reconciliation might look like: *Ubuntu*. He writes, "*Ubuntu* is very difficult to render into western language. It speaks of the very essence of being human... It is to say: 'My humanity is caught up in and inextricably bound up in yours.' We belong in a bundle of life; we say, 'A person is a person through other persons.' It is not: 'I think, therefore I am.' It says rather, 'I am human because I belong. I participate. I share'" (Tutu, p. 31).

When I read that, I started thinking to myself, how much that French dude, Rene Descartes, has dictated our identity: "I think, therefore I am." Such a world creates a world of thinking individuals, but what about community?"

But what if I am, because of you, and because of me, you are, and because of us, we're we? That just because we're human. God's creation is enough bond to hold us together. Paul proclaims here in Ephesians, and in other letters, that a new human being was made in Christ, where such distinctions as

Gentile and Jew have been tossed aside. That new human has *Ubuntu*---that connection, that creative connection that God has placed in all of us. It's as if Paul says this new human has the qualities of *Ubuntu*. This new human is open and available to others, affirming of others, does not feel threatened. Paul's new humanity says that others are able and good, for he or she has a proper self-assurance that comes from knowing that she belongs to a greater whole and is diminished when others are humiliated or diminished, when others are tortured, or oppressed, or treated as if they are less than who they are.

I think in some ways what Paul is talking about is reflected in this word *Ubuntu*. He calls forth a community of faith surrounded by the presence of Christ that is seeking to bring a new humanity. A humanity where the lines of distinction are blurred. Where we care for one another; we carry each other's burdens; we love, are patient and generous with one another. As we gather together; we seek to affirm that which holds us together rather than dwelling on that which tears us apart. "*Ubuntu*" – it's a word that spoke to me; maybe it will to you. Amen

Chapter Sources

Barth, Markus. <u>Ephesians 4-6,</u> The Anchor Bible. Garden City, NY: Doubleday and Co. Inc., 1974.

Tutu, Desmond. <u>No Future Without Forgiveness</u>. New York: Image, Doubleday, 2000.

Ward, Richard. <u>Feasting on the Word</u>, Year B, Vol. 3, Edited by David L. Bartlett and Barbara Brown Taylor. Louisville, KY: Westminster/John Knox Press, 2009.

Chapter 7

Equipped to Serve

Introduction

It is easy in our very complex world to forget the importance of each person in the church. We live in a culture that celebrates celebrities and leadership. Thus, it is not uncommon for people in the church to focus on the pastor or pastors, lay leaders, or anyone who stands before the community of faith as a focal point. Today's scripture calls us back to the basics. The church as the body of Christ is truly the church when everyone realizes their importance. Paul uses a term which implies the critical nature of this basic connection. This term will be the focal point of our message.

Scripture: Ephesians 4:7-16

"But each of us was given grace according to the measure of Christ's gift. Therefore it is said, 'When he ascended on high, he made captivity itself a captive; he gave gifts to his people.' (When it says, 'He ascended,' what does it mean but that he had also descended into the lower parts of the earth? He who descended is the same one who ascended far above all the heavens, so that he might fill all things.) The gifts he gave were that some would be apostles, some prophets, some evangelists, some pastors and teachers, to equip the saints for the work of ministry, for building up the body of Christ, until all of us come to the unity of the faith and of the knowledge of the Son of God, to maturity, to the measure of the full stature of Christ. We must no longer be children, tossed to and fro and blown about by every wind of doctrine, by people's trickery, by their craftiness in deceitful scheming. But speaking the truth in love, we must grow up in every way into him who is the head, into Christ, from whom the whole body, joined and knit together by every ligament with which it is equipped, as each part is working properly, promotes the body's growth in building itself up in love" (Ephesians 4:7-16, NRSV).

Sermon

One of the most evocative and powerful images of the church was created by Paul in his letter to the church in Corinth. He called the church "the body of Christ." And in that letter, he used that image to address two concerns. The first concern was that there were certain members who felt they were more important than others. Paul said: "How can the head say to the feet I have no use of you?" Such a statement would be ridiculous. The second concern centered on some internal factions and so Paul says: there's a connectivity to the body. If one part of the body hurts, the rest of the body hurts. If one part of the body rejoices, the rest of the body rejoices. What makes this metaphor, or image so powerful, is simply that it is true! What individual would go around saying: "I don't want to have a foot?" Or, "I don't want to have a hand?" All parts of our body are important and when some part of our body becomes decompensated, we realize how much we depend on it. We've all stubbed our toe and even though the toe may be small, the whole body feels the pain. It is the concept of connectivity that Paul carries into this letter to the church in Ephesus. We are the body of Christ and we are connected. He shifts it a little bit in that he creates the head of the body as being Jesus Christ and talks about some unique ways that we grow, but he still uses this body metaphor which I think is so very important.

He begins by asserting in verse 7, that we have been given "gifts"; actually, we have been given "grace". He gets to the gifts after his little bible study on gifts in verses 8-10. These verses are very detailed and technical, and since this is not a bible study I will just sum up verses 8-10: God gave you gifts. So, by grace, we have been given gifts--each one of us. I think this is complimentary to the passage that we read last week where Paul states that we are one. We are unified together, but unity does not necessarily mean uniformity. So we have unity, we are one body. But we at the same time have diversity; we have many different gifts that are a part of the body. Paul doesn't say these gifts are parceled out on an egalitarian basis. It's as if God knows exactly the gifts that we need, and God gives us those gifts. Now I've met some folks who are so busy doing other things that they have not practiced using some of those gifts God has given them. So, part of our process is discovering the gifts, but that is not the purpose of this sermon today. Rather let's acknowledge the very fact that God has given us gifts and these gifts are based upon God's grace and that each one of us has been given gifts as God sees fit.

These gifts are not ends unto themselves--they are things that help us do something. I like the way Marcus Barth, in his commentary states, "The saints experience God's good will, power and presence by receiving grace – the grace given is neither a pillow for sleeping nor a comfortable, warm feeling, but a ministry. It is a privilege implying responsibility and action" (p. 430).

The gifts are given to each member of the body of Christ for some kind of action. That action in this text is that we equip the saints for ministry. I also like what Barth says about that little word: equip. The Greek noun for equip is *katartismos*; it occurs only here in the New Testament. It is derived from a verb that means "to reconcile between political parties" (that is not the sermon today)--"to set bones as in a surgery" (nope that is not the sermon today either)--or more generally, "to restore, to prepare, or to create." Ah that's the sermon- "to restore", "to prepare" or "to create." The noun describes the dynamic act by which persons or things are properly conditioned. In other words, God has given the body gifts so that the body through each individual member can use those gifts to prepare the body for ministry.

What does that ministry look like? What does the ministry focus on? He says it focuses on a unity of the faith and the knowledge of Jesus. Well, what good will that do? Paul says that when we have the unity of the faith and we are beginning the process of knowing Jesus, we become mature. The actual Greek phrase is fascinating, it is *andres telios*. Literally, it can be translated a "perfect human being." I've never liked *telios* being translated "perfect," especially in a biblical context. *Telios* can also be translated "complete, full, filled with purpose." So Paul is saying when the church is functioning, it's unified in its faith; it's seeking to know Jesus. In the process of knowing Jesus, it's growing, it's maturing, it's fulfilling its purpose; it's coming to its end and when will we know that this process is complete? Paul says, when the church and each one of you looks like Jesus.

Our measure is not just Jesus, but the full stature of Jesus. I don't know about you, but I love abstract thoughts, and this particular passage could be something to think about and contemplate on all day long. This is great stuff. Equip the saints for the unity of the faith. Know Jesus and mature in the faith.

Let me give two practical implications from this very lofty sermon. The first implication is there is no word "retirement" in discipleship. We have to strike that word from our vocabulary. I get a lot of people saying, "Well pastor, I'm retired." Outside this church that matters; inside this church, I don't know what that word means because Paul says we are the body of Christ and each one of us has been gifted and we need to build up the body. We need to equip saints for ministry until everyone around us, including ourselves in the church in general looks like Jesus We have a long way to go, my friends. I have a feeling we'll be doing this activity until we see Jesus again--so there is no retirement in ministry. We are called to be the body of Christ until we die and are welcomed into the Kingdom. It's a life-long discipleship.

Another practical implication from this reality is discussed in verse 14. When we are maturing, when we are reaching our purpose, when we are coming to our end goal, our faith becomes centered and settled. We're no longer tossed to and fro'. It is important to understand in this text that Paul is primarily talking to the church, not to individuals. He sees the church tossed to and fro', going this way and going that way, and if you think that that was just hyperbole, read First Corinthians. The church in that epistle was tossed to and fro' all over the place as a community of faith.

As we grow and mature, we find our equilibrium because the church that is maturing realizes that Jesus is in the center of everything that we do. Now that would seem to be an obvious statement for the members of the church to make. But I am always amazed that we who have inherited 1600 years of Christendom, regularly assume Jesus must be around, but in our act of assuming, we quickly forget that Jesus really is at the center of all we do. Instead we often create church activities that have little to do with the ministry that Jesus has called us to enact.

This reminds me of what Ruben Welch says in his book, *We Really Do Need Each Other.* "There's a difference between the fellowship of Christians and Christian Fellowship" (p. 39). Reuben states that the distinction is this, the fellowship of

Christians is any gathering of a bunch of like-minded Jesus followers who like hanging out. Christian Fellowship is a community that is committed to showing the world what it means to be a community, how to forgive one another, how to talk to one another in difficult times. It's ultimately a fellowship in which the world says, "I've never seen anything like that." If the church looks no more than a replica of daily life, most people are going to ignore us. When the church, in its process of maturity, begins to understand that Christ is at the center of everything we do, then we begin to become more focused. Jesus becomes the center of all that we do.

Paul says when true Christian fellowship happens there are two things that need to occur. The first one concerns speaking truth to one another in love. I'm not going to talk about this for another two weeks. In addition to speaking the truth in love, we're called to grow into Christ who is our head. Now that's an odd thing. We usually think of growth coming from the head down but we're going to grow into Christ. I tried to find some kind of an example of this and this is the best I came up with. It's like when you have a little baby and often times I've seen this, where the head of the baby is large and we often times comment, "They'll 'grow' into it." What we mean is that the proportion of the head to the body will change. They will eventually balance out. That same image of "growing into it," may be related to what Paul is saying. Christ is our head, and as we mature, we grow into Christ and so the head of Christ gives a shape and form; it helps us understand what it means to be a mature Christian. So we grow into Christ.

Paul says the way that the body grows into Christ is when the body realizes that it has a connectivity within the body. Paul states that through the body's joints and ligaments there is a connection at a very fundamental level. The Spirit is able to flow through the body when all of these parts are together or in contact. I'm utterly fascinated by that word "ligament.". In the Greek it's called *haphes*. Aristotle used the word *haphes* to describe his physiology of the human being. Aristotle believed that within our body, there are millions of little *haphes*--little points of connection. And when one of those *haphes* gets dislodged, everything after it can no longer receive nutrition. Thus, Aristotle is saying "You don't have an elbow if you don't have a bunch of *haphes* between the shoulder and the elbow, and you don't have a functional hand unless you've got a bunch of *haphes* between your elbow and your hand. These little teeny connections allow the body to function." When we take this concept in a spiritual way, which I think Paul is implying, then we understand the church as made up of little *haphes*, little points of connection.

Now, we can get fooled. We sometimes think that what's important to our body is our hands, our elbows, our shoulders--it's the same in the church. Sometimes we think what's important in the church is the pastor, the staff, and the elders. Well, those folks are important, but they are not the church. They are not what makes the church BE the church. It's every little *haphes*. Every little point of connection. That's all of us. Connected, gifted--to equip the body. But unless we know that we are important, we may drop off--and guess what? A part of the body becomes dysfunctional. Have you ever been in a church where the lights were on, the music was playing, worship happened, but there was no life? This is a church whose *haphes* have lost their connectivity. The body functions, but it's limping. What is being pictured here is the body of Christ, fully functioning, filled with the Spirit flowing through the body as each *haphes* is in connection.

So, here's your task for this week if not next week. There are a bunch of *haphes* in this church. I want you to have "*haphes* eyes", and when you see somebody do something, maybe small, maybe big, maybe something inconsequential, maybe something very consequential, I want you to connect with them in one of five ways: talk to them, email them, text them, voicemail or telephone or send them a letter. And in that communication, I want you to simply say: "I noticed what you did – this church is the church because of you." Every *haphes*, every person--it could be someone who simply turns around to you in worship and says, "how has your week been?" And when you share, you realize they really want to know. It could be someone who offers you a word of encouragement. It could be someone who teaches a Sunday School class; it could be someone who has led in worship; it could be those who shared with music – we've got all of these *haphes* and I just simply want you to recognize them and point them out. Not to somehow place undo focus on the person, but to let them know they are a part of that connectivity that allows the body of Christ to function as God has intended us to function. Amen

Sources

Barth, Marcus. Ephesians 4-6. Anchor Bible. Garden City, New York: Doubleday and Co., Inc., 1974.

Welch, Reuben. We Really Do Need Each Other. Nashville, TN: Impact Books, 1982.

Chapter 8

Practicing the Faith

Introduction

The sacrament of baptism is an action of the church that has deep and theological meaning. Yet, in our secularized society, it has often been reduced to a beautiful moment with a baby and a family. Our text today uses the imagery of baptism to talk about the radical change implied in our call to follow Christ. It is a call that we especially need in this day.

Scripture: Ephesians 4:17-24

"Now this I affirm and insist on in the Lord: you must no longer live as the Gentiles live, in the futility of their minds. They are darkened in their understanding, alienated from the life of God because of their ignorance and hardness of heart. They have lost all sensitivity and have abandoned themselves to licentiousness, greedy to practice every kind of impurity. That is not the way you learned Christ! For surely you have heard about him and were taught in him, as truth is in Jesus. You were taught to put away your former way of life, your old self, corrupt and deluded by its lusts, and to be renewed in the spirit of your minds, and to clothe yourselves with the new self, created according to the likeness of God in true righteousness and holiness" (Ephesians 4:17-24, NRSV).

Sermon

As some of you know, we have been in a series of sermons going through the Book of Ephesians since September. Now we're about halfway through so it's time for your test.

Everybody gets out your pen and paper and we'll do a little review--not really. I think a little review of where we've been will help us understand exactly what Paul is doing at this part of the letter.

In Chapter 1, Paul announces that in Jesus Christ something amazing has happened. We have been blessed by the presence of Christ who has revealed to us a secret that God had planned since the beginning of the ages: namely that Gentiles are a part of God's salvific plan.

In Chapter 2, Paul began to talk about those Gentiles who were part of the Ephesian church. He shared with them that they as well as all others, are a part of the church through the grace of God. The church is a place in which the barriers, the distinctions that had separated the Jews from Gentiles for millennia, had been abolished in Christ. God was in the process of creating a new kind of person, a new humanity and it was the church's calling to live that humanity out.

Then, in Chapter 4, Paul begins to articulate what this calling will look like. What does the new humanity in Christ look like? And so for two Sundays we have looked at two of those images: that we are unified in our faith and that we are connected to Christ who is the head of the church. This Sunday and next we will look at two other images--namely transformation and renewal. We are to be a people who are transformed and renewed.

The imagery used by Paul towards the end of this passage is clearly baptismal imagery. As soon as we talk about baptism, we need to adjust our thoughts. What the Ephesians understood baptism to be was radically different from how we may have experienced baptism in our own lives. So if you've been raised in a mainline church, baptism is usually as follows.

In the middle of the worship service, the pastor comes to the baptismal font and parents bring a child, usually a young child, maybe even an infant. They make a statement of faith and they, and the congregation promise to raise this child in the faith. Water is placed on the child's head--children either think that is wonderful, or they let everybody know they are not happy about all this wetness--a prayer is given. It is a significant moment in the life of the family and the life of the congregation. That was not the context of baptism in Ephesus.

First, these Ephesians were not raised in Christian homes--they were Gentiles. Secondly, these Gentiles were not raised in a nation, or a culture that had been shaped and formed by 1600 years of Christians being in charge. They were Gentiles. They were pagan. Christianity was this little teeny sect that had no voice in society and was of little concern. And so, when they became Christians, when they were baptized, a radical transformation was understood by all.

Paul goes out of his way to paint a fairly dreary picture of who they once were. They had minds that were futile and darkened. That word "futile" can mean "empty" or "without purpose." I like the way the Jerusalem Bible phrases it: "They lived an aimless life." If you've ever lived an aimless life or have seen people in an aimless way of being, it's not a great way to be. They were a people who were apart from the life of God. Paul articulates this more clearly in Chapter 2 where he says the Gentiles did not inherit the covenant of God, the Torah, the blessings that God had given the people of Israel, and so they were apart from what God's purpose was for humans. And finally their hearts were hardened. I like this translation--they had "petrified hearts." It's an Old Testament phrase that talks about somebody who really is not aware of God's presence or doesn't allow God's voice to make any difference in life--their hearts are hardened. Paul clearly states that because of all of these realities they end up living their life amidst greed, licentiousness and impurity. They lived as they wanted to live, they did what they wanted to do, whenever they wanted to do it. No one sensed any type of limits in how they lived their life, this is Paul's perspective.

I appreciated what Pheme Perkins says in her commentary, when she notes that as you read this section of the text, amidst this cascading description of the Gentile lives, Paul seeks to talk to our emotions rather than just adding information (p. 428). You've heard speeches like that, where the words of the speaker cascade down and your mind begins to be overloaded. But if it's done well, your heart begins to be moved. And that's what Paul is trying to do—He's saying your life as a Gentile is such a radically different life than the life you are called to be now as Christian.

This transformation occurred for these young Christians, in what Marcus Barth calls "The School of the Messiah." Paul just simply says, "You were taught Jesus." I like what Barth says concerning this concept, "…the author of Ephesians intended to present Christ as a message and a teacher – a lesson and a school at the same time. In the Messiah school the medium and the message are not only inseparable but completely identified. Here indeed the medium is the message. Why and when can a school effect as great a change as liberation from futile gentile ways? The answer is this: When Jesus Christ is the Headmaster, the teaching matter, the method, the curriculum and the academy then the gift of new life takes the place of a diploma" (p. 530)

I like that imagery. Christ becomes the Headmaster and the curriculum so that everything you do, and are, is Jesus. When this occurred in the lives of these Ephesian Christians it was a major break from everyday life. In fact, the church believed it was going to be such a big break that when one was exploring the possibility of becoming Christian in some places the church gave individuals up to three years to prepare. And so you went through a series of classes. Not just teaching you the faith but teaching you a different way of being. One of the things our Wednesday bible study looked at in Paul's first letter to the church in Corinth, is that Paul told folks that they couldn't go to the assembly halls where idols were in abundance. One of the biblical interpreters of I Corinthians said that these "temples" were actually a place where everyday business was done. Think of it as membership in a country club or hanging out at the bar. It was just a common place where people went to do business. And so what Paul is saying is when you become a Christian, all of those connections you have in the business world have got to stop. Now if I were a business person, I think I would object to that: "Paul, I'm not worshipping any idols, I'm just making connections in the business world." Paul says: "You're a Christian now. Things are different."

So, it took up to three years for the transformation, a reorientation for these Gentiles moving into the Christian way of being. Then, when they were baptized, almost all of them were baptized at the same time on Easter Sunday. They would gather together with a small community of faith. Then they would walk into the worship space wearing an old garb-- something that represented their old life, maybe a cloak that represented the way they once were. When they got into the church, they literally took that cloak off and they were naked. They then proceeded into the baptismal, not a font, but a pool where they were completely immersed. As soon as they came up out of that water there was a brother or sister in Christ who had a white cloak, brand new, and they would place it on their bodies. This is the imagery of putting away, or taking off and putting on, or being clothed in Jesus that Paul so frequently uses.

I think is a powerful image. We all know the importance of clothes in our life. We used to say, "Clothes make the man or woman." I don't know if they say that anymore but I do know that it takes some time for my wife to decide what she's going to wear based on what she's going to do. While I pride myself in not taking so much time, I too, pay attention to my clothing and the event I am attending. So, I think it still matters what we wear; what we wear portrays who we are at any given moment. And so I think this imagery of taking off that which was old and putting on that which was new is a very powerful metaphor.

Paul says that all of this change is a process; baptism happens once, but then the implications of baptism are a process. If you look at the verbs in verses 22, 23 and 24, there are three of them and they are all in the Greek infinitive form. The verbs "to take or to put off" and "to put on or to clothe yourself," are all in the Greek Aorist tense, which means an action that is completed. It's that middle verb that I find most amazing. The middle verb is in the present tense; so you've put off, you've put on, and the middle verb says you are now in the process of renewing your Spirit--and that's an ongoing process. The act of baptism includes the one time acts of taking off and putting on. Both of these are enacted one time, that part of the process is over with; now comes the renewal. And that is a process that takes quite a bit of time.

This got me thinking, maybe some of you have had this kind of transformation? Maybe there was a point in your life where you had a certain profession or job that required you to wear clothing that identified you with a particular profession. And then you switched professions or jobs and you had to wear something radically different. Let's say you wore a basic workman's uniform and then you were wearing a suit and tie. That transition is fairly easy--one day you're wearing an outfit that's for a workman and the next day you are wearing a suit. But it takes a little while to try to figure out what the implications are of wearing a suit? That transition takes a while. The reality of changing clothes can happen quickly, but the transition takes a while. We've got to work ourselves into that new reality. That's what happened to these Gentiles. They were used to this way of being that had been taken off, they'd put on something new and now they were in the process of constant renewal. It's an ongoing process and Paul says in that renewal you will be a people who will be righteous like God. In other words, you will be in right relationship with God and you will also be holy. You will be set aside for God's purposes. This is who you are becoming. This person who has changed clothing to become more like God.

Now, the question I ask myself is, how can this kind of imagery work in a context where most of us did not have a radical break from one way of life to become a Christian? Maybe some of you did. But if you are like many I know, you were raised probably like myself, in a Christian home and to become a Christian was just like being a part of the family. I mean the biggest decision now is whether you go to church on Sunday or not. Or which church will you attend? There's not that significant, radical break. So, how can this message really speak to us? What's the practical implication? For me, it is the image of taking off and putting on. The transformation doesn't have to be a radical experience, but I think it can be something that can have radical implications.

Let's use some of the imagery of Ephesians to bring it home. We live in a world in which the divisions, distinctions, and the distances and the particularities of people are always before us. The difference between men and women, the difference between someone who lives in the country and someone who lives in the city, the difference between a Republican and Democrat, the difference between someone who is a blue collar worker and a white collar worker, the difference between someone born in the United States and someone who is an immigrant to the United States, difference between skin color, economic status--it's in our face all the time! I believe this text says we have got to put away that type of thinking, that kind of view of the world, where these distinctions create divisions. Such a perspective is to be put away because in Christ, as Paul says in Galatians, there is no more Jew or Gentile, there is no more male or female, there is no slave or free, we are all one in Christ (Galatians 3:28).

We must put on a new identity that no longer sees those arbitrary distinctions that divide us. I think that is a message that will need to reside in our hearts for some time. Beginning by being a community that no longer sees the world as being divided over differences between Jew and Gentile, insider or outsider, but a community who simply sees the world as filled with God's children, some who have wandered away and apart from God's purpose and promise. And may the others of us who are limping along trying to follow Jesus as best as we can, invite them to be a part of that journey, to be a part of that process of taking off those distinctions that divide us and putting on a reality that calls us to be one. Amen.

Chapter Sources

Barth, Markus. Ephesians 4-6, The Anchor Bible. Garden City, New York: Doubleday and Company, Inc., 1974.

Perkins, Pheme. <u>Ephesians</u> (Vol. XI), in The New Interpreter's Bible. Nashville: Abingdon Press, 2000.

The Jerusalem Bible. Garden City, New York: Doubleday & Company, Inc., 1966.

Chapter 9

Some Basic Rules for the New Life

Introduction

While much of the material we have been reading in this section of the book of Ephesians has been very practical, this particular section changes directions. Paul offers five basic rules for the new life of a baptized Christian. In addition to the rules, he provides theological motives as well. The sermon places a keen interest in those motives, for in them we find the true gem of Paul's mind. This is more than just a session on "Do's" and "Don'ts"; it is a deeply pastoral section that seeks to address rules for community living that are firmly grounded in good theology.

Scripture: Ephesians 4:25-5:1

"So then, putting away falsehood, let all of us speak the truth to our neighbors, for we are members of one another. Be angry but do not sin; do not let the sun go down on your anger, and do not make room for the devil. Thieves must give up stealing; rather let them labor and work honestly with their own hands, so as to have something to share with the needy. Let no evil talk come out of your mouths, but only what is useful for building up, as there is need, so that your words may give grace to those who hear. And do not grieve the Holy Spirit of God, with which you were marked with a seal for the day of redemption. Put away from you all bitterness and wrath and anger and wrangling and slander, together with all malice, and be kind to one another, tenderhearted, forgiving one another, as God in Christ has forgiven you. Therefore be imitators of God, as beloved children, and live in love, as Christ loved us and gave himself up for us, a fragrant offering and sacrifice to God" (Ephesians 4:25 – 5:1, NRSV).

Sermon

You remember last week that Paul talked about how we need to be renewed and transformed to be part of this new humanity that God is creating in Jesus Christ. He used baptismal imagery, specifically the moment in their baptism when each individual took off their old clothes, was baptized and then--emerging from the water--put on a new robe to indicate their new life in Christ.

Paul now articulates what that act of taking off and putting on looks like in daily life through a series of five guidelines, or five basic rules, for this new life. They are presented in a tri-partite grid that looks like this. It begins with a prohibition – something you need to <u>stop</u> doing. It continues with a commandment--there's something you need to <u>start</u> doing. Then the most fascinating thing in this section is, we're given a motive.

How many times in life, when we are urged to change, are we not really given good motives? Like when we're kids, when told to do something that we don't want to do...well why? "Because your mama said so." That doesn't work really well for a child. Or sometimes you may remember at work when someone in management said you needed to change. And the reason why? "Do you want to work here tomorrow"? These are not good motives. They may work for a while, but they are not the kind of motive that really nurtures us, that cause us to truly change from the inside. In contrast to those examples, Paul provides compelling motives to his readers. I believe these motives are the best part of this letter written by Paul to the church in Ephesus. We are going to look at these five rules, especially concentrating on the motives because they provide a depth of meaning that is not provided solely by a prohibition and command.

Number one, the Ephesians are to stop lying, or as our text says: "stop all falsehood." Let's talk a little bit about that for a moment.

The command, then, is to begin to speak the truth to one another and the motive for that is this: they are members one of another; and they are a community that's deeply connected. When I say that they should stop lying I don't necessarily think that Paul intends a simple kind of lie -- just not telling the truth. But a broader kind of lying, and maybe this is where "falsehood" is actually a better translation. In the Greek, it is *pseudos*--don't be *pseudos*, don't be fake. So, there's a certain sense of integrity here. We are called to put aside that sort of falsehood that has no integrity and put on that which is truthful. And we do this because we are a community. Alan Verhey, in his commentary on this particular passage, says, "No genuine community can be built on deception; it must be built on the truth. This community, the church, is to be built on the truth of Jesus and it is to be marked by truthfulness. The intimate connection of truth telling, and community works both ways. Truth telling nurtures genuine community and genuine community nurtures truth telling" (Verhey, p. 188).

I think that's true. But we all know how hard it is in church to do that. In fact, many of us believe that this is the one place you don't want to be real. You might put on a façade--"How are things going?" "Oh just fine, no need to pray for me; I'm doing great." I'm not saying that we're all in a Gestalt moment at church where we bare our whole soul. What I'm talking about is a community, with the sense that the reason we are here, lies in the fact we want to be honest with our lives. I think the call to confession and the prayer of confession, are both a weekly reminder of our need to just simply speak the truth to ourselves and to one another. I think the closest example of this is the presence of 12-Step groups that meet on our campus, and isn't it interesting that most 12-Step groups are associated with churches? It's almost like they're reminding us "this is how you ought to be." I love the way Fredrick Buechner describes this process in his *Telling Secrets*: "They are sitting in the basement of a church [most of you know what a basement is, right?] Have any of you been in the basement of a church? That sort of damp, dank smell, fluorescent lights buzzing overhead, yes, that's there too...there is an urn of coffee, there is a basket which is passed around at some point into which everybody who can afford to puts a dollar to help pay for the coffee and the rent of the room.

"In one sense, they are strangers who know each other only by their first names and almost nothing else about each other. In another sense, they are best friends who little by little come to know each other from the inside out, instead of the other way around which is the way we usually do it...

"They could hardly be a more ill-assorted lot. Some are educated and some never finished grade school. Some are on welfare and some have hit the jackpot. Some are straight and some are gay. There are senior citizens among them; also twenty-year olds. Some groups are composed of alcoholics and some like the ones I found my way to are people who have not alcoholic problems themselves but come from families who did. The one thing they have in common can be easily stated. It is just that they all believe they cannot live fully human lives without each other and without what they call their 'higher power.'" (pp. 89-91)

Now, I am not asking that the church become a 12-Step group. But it seems this is a group which understands that while they don't need to share all the secrets of their souls in order to be honest, they have learned that the only reason for getting together is to be honest about their lives. They know that they have lived their life in dishonesty for too long. They know that when they are honest with their life, they need to be around other people who are honest with their lives. And I think it's telling that they tend to hang out in churches, just to say, maybe somewhere in the vestige of this place what we are doing, being honest about our lives is best done in a church building where living in honesty can be real. Because the community of faith can only be a community when it's honest. When it lives, it lives the truth--Rule number 1.

Rule number 2: I have summarized this as--stop destructive anger. The command is to deal with our anger in the now; "don't let the sun go down on your anger". And the motivation, (this may not work for many Presbyterians, but it is the truth)--that unresolved anger is the devil's workshop.

Now, Paul could have simply said "Don't be angry." But he is human enough to know that anger actually can be a very positive part of our life. There can be a kind of anger that rises up in us when we see injustice. It is that kind of anger that says, "I'm motivated to do something to change this. I want to make this better, I want to bring justice." In this way anger can be funneled in a very positive direction.

What Paul is talking about is the kind of anger that becomes a cesspool. It is an anger that lives within us and may also lead us to a place in which we actually begin to enjoy our anger. Once again Buechner speaks vividly about this kind of anger. This particular quote has been one of my favorite Buechner sayings. In fact, I read this back in the 1980s and it still speaks a deep truth to me. This is Buechner's definition of anger, "Of the seven deadly sins, anger is possibly the most fun. To lick your wounds, to smack your lips over grievances long past, to roll your tongue over the prospect for bitter confrontations still to come, to savor to the last toothsome morsel, both the pain you are given and the pain you are giving back. In many ways, it is a feast fit for a king. The chief drawback is that what you are wolfing down is yourself; the skeleton at the feast is you" (Wishful Thinking, p. 2).

I think such destructive uses of anger can happen to both individuals and communities. When we revel in our anger, it can easily become a cesspool for the devil's use--"But ours is righteous anger!!" Unless our anger is funneled into the key acts of justice, it's going to become a cesspool of embitteredness. And I think Buechner was right--we've all been there a few times, where the prospect of letting go of that anger doesn't seem like that much fun. There's a part of us that holds on to it even when we know it is destroying us. We just can't let it go. Paul says community cannot be built with people who hold on to that kind of anger, who fester that kind of anger; who feed on that kind of anger.

You may have heard of this church out of Wichita, Kansas, that goes around to funerals and other places and says some unbelievably destructive, derogatory things to folks because they're "speaking the truth and saying what God says to the world." I don't think they've read their bible well. We need to let go of anger. And that anger we feel when we see injustice? Let's funnel it into action; let's do something to steer that anger into making a difference in the world.

Number three: this one's an odd one: "Stop stealing, work honestly." I love the motivation--"so that you can give to others." Stop stealing. Was this church filled with thieves and con artists? It seems odd--where's the protestant work ethic when you need it? Right?--A bunch of people not really wanting to work hard for what they get? I think it goes deeper than that. Fowl gives some options both in what he thought Paul might be saying to the Ephesian congregation as well as some things that might apply to us. The first thing I think Paul is talking about includes the numerous small-scale ways in which slaves might pilfer their masters' goods because there were a lot of slaves in these early church communities and they might take a little bit here and there. Many of you have worked in an office; you see something you need and rationalize that the office doesn't really need these things; they'd be better at my house. I do work at home any way so...you know...that kind of pilfering. In addition, Paul might be referring to those in the marketplace who use unfair scales or engage in price fixing...unfortunately, that has been a reality since the days of the Old Testament. Petty con-artists might also have fit the bill (p. 157).

A second possible situation could be present., In light of the manifest fact that this entire passage is addressed to the common life of the Ephesian church, the reader must entertain the likelihood that those stealing are stealing from other members of the congregation. In Paul's letter to the Corinthians he states that members of the community should no longer go to lawyers. Such a prohibition was given because wealthy Corinthians were most likely taking their poor Corinthian brothers and sisters to court because they could afford a lawyer and they knew the weaker ones or poorer ones couldn't. They justified their actions by saying "Well, our fellow Christians have broken the law." And Paul says, "It's destroying the community! You're stealing from one another. We've got to stop this."

What I find interesting is the motive. You would think if Paul was a man shaped by the Protestant work ethic, he would say, "stop stealing, work honestly." The motivation--so that you can provide for your family as well as the security of your future. Right? But Paul has done something else. You see we tend to think of good work as a private kind of thing, a virtue. We work hard to build good character, and that's all good and fine. But it's all about us, and Paul is saying, "No, you need to work so you can provide for others." It's a social motive; it's a communal work ethic. So, he's calling us as a baptized people to understand this basic biblical principle, that wages we receive from working are never ours. It is a gift from God. Unfortunately, when it becomes ours, we tend to hoard it or misuse it. But when we understand that it is a gift from God, we actually use it wisely, enjoy it and share it. That's what the baptized life is all about. Working hard, not trying to defraud anyone and sharing it with those around you.

Number four: our text says, "Stop evil speech," but that's not the best translation, especially because I think too many can slide away from the extreme image of "evil speech." I liked when someone called it "corrosive speech." The Greek word is *sapras* and that doesn't mean evil. It means words that are rotten, words that degrade and defile. Although no major translator defines this word as "corrosive speech," but that does not mean such a translation is inaccurate. We know what kind of speech Paul is talking about, the drip, drip, drip, rusting kind of speech that just continues to wear someone down. Paul calls us to stop such speech because we need to speak words that edify or build one another up. I love this motive – who doesn't want to receive grace when someone speaks to them?

This kind of speech doesn't mean that we can't confront each other on important matters. But we do it with a sense of caring and love with the intention of building someone up, not just believing that we need to tell them the truth. This should be a relational kind of sharing and thus, when you have harsh words or difficult things to say to people you love, I would advise no emails or texting of those things because they need to see you. They need to receive the grace that comes from you as you are seeking to enact a difficult sharing. In emails and texting, they just "read" the data. We need to be a people who understand, that most of the time what we need to do is speak grace-filled words. Because I want to hear grace-filled words in the morning, in the afternoon and in the evening, so why shouldn't I offer grace-filled words to you?

When I was working on this sermon, I thought of the Richard Rohr classes. Some of you who have attend the Richard Rohr classes may recognize this [I hope some of you do, that way I'll know you've been paying attention to what I've said]. Rohr states "There are three gates through which a wise man's word must pass. One: Is what I am saying really true? If it's not true, then why bother? Two: Is it loving? Am I about to say something that will build up life and trust, or will it tear both of them down? And three: [And this is my favorite] Is what I am about to say really necessary? If it's not, why clutter up the moment with more words and noise competing for space and attention" (p. 85).

Don't you love that? I mean, what Rohr is talking about, what Paul is talking about is that speech matters. The way we speak, how we speak, what we speak--it matters. The only way we can be a community, the only way to be a people centered in the life of Jesus, is to build each other up. That doesn't mean we don't confront one another with difficult discussions, but we do it in a relationally loving, caring way. We live in a culture that spews out so much venom simply because we can. We say,

"I'm just being me, it's how I feel"--and we're destroying ourselves. Good law. Good rule. We need to start practicing it.

The last rule: there's a list of vices here, I'll call them the progressive power of vices: bitterness, wrath, anger, wrangling, slander and malice. If you look at these, they actually intensify. They start from inside a person and then they progress out. Once they go out, they cause what I call group toxicity -- bitterness, wrath, anger, now wrangling, and then slander, and finally malice. It is a formula for the destruction of community and life together. No wonder Paul wants us to take these actions away from our life.

In contrast, Paul says what we need to put on is tenderness, compassion and forgiveness. And here the motive is one that we cannot escape. What motivates us to be compassionate or forgiving to one another? Is it because we're really nice people? No, it's because that's the way God has treated us. The truth, my friends, is that before you ever knew who you were, God loved you. Before you ever chose Christ, He chose you. Paul says in Romans, while we were yet sinners Christ died for us (Romans 5:8). This unbelievable, relentless love of Jesus is given to us before we can do anything ourselves. And because of Christ's love for us we find ourselves without much of a choice here, do we? Because none of us wants to return kindness, forgiveness and compassion with hatred, vitriol and destructiveness. You might think but Lord!! They deserve it!! So did you. And guess what happened to you? Someone was kind to you, loved you, was compassionate toward you, forgave you.

My friends, I wish I could give us a little bit of give on this one, but this is the bottom line--God loves us and God has forgiven us. In other words, we can't truly take our baptism seriously without taking seriously that we must live with others the way

God has lived with us. That's why Paul summarizes this whole thing by saying [if you somehow missed it] just imitate God. Just imitate God. This is surprising, because when Paul says, "imitate God," this is the only place where this particular exhortation is found in the whole of the New Testament. And that's really interesting…we're never asked to imitate God except here. And so I conclude with this insight from Verhey who comments "We are to imitate God by practicing kindness, compassion and forgiveness as God in Christ has forgiven us. We are to imitate God as beloved children. Every parent knows, to their shame sometimes, how children learn to speak and to act by imitating their parents. God's actions and dispositions are a model for God's beloved children to follow because to be beloved by God is to have a model for love of a neighbor. We are to imitate God is the climactic conclusion of this section, which states that by living in love as a way of life we find a common life that is marked by love" (p. 206).

Do you begin to understand that this word of love is a repetitive word, one we have heard over and over in Ephesians. Love. It reminds me of a preacher who was new to a church and the first Sunday he preached on love and the second Sunday he preached on love and the third Sunday he preached on love and finally an elder came up to him and said, "Pastor do you have any other sermons?" And the pastor said, "As soon as you listen to this first one, I'll move on to sermon number two." It's one of those truths we cannot escape.

So what are the five basic rules of the new life? Four out of the five have to do with the way we talk to one another. So, be mindful, my friends, the Book of James says the tongue is a powerful tool. That same tongue can build up and edify as well as tear down and destroy. Remember that you are baptized members of the Body of Christ. You are part of the family of

God who has shown you nothing but kindness, compassion, mercy and forgiveness. Let us go out and live this kind of reality. Amen.

Chapter Sources

Buechner, Frederick. Telling Secrets. San Francisco: HarperSan Francisco, 1991)

Buechner, Frederick. Wishful Thinking. New York: Harper and Row Publishers, 1973.

Fowl, Stephen. Ephesians. The New Testament Library. Louisville, KY: Westminster/John Knox Press, 2012.

Rohr, Richard. On the Threshold of Transformation. Chicago: Loyola Press, 2010.

Verhey, Allen and Joseph S. Harvard. Ephesians, Belief, Louisville, KY: Westminster/John Knox Press, 2011.

Chapter 10

The Trouble with Submission

Introduction

This sermon is my attempt to wade through a difficult text. It seeks to truly hear what Paul was saying to Christians centuries ago, while still attempting to hear what the Spirit may say to us. It is a conversation we need to have more often.

I have entitled this sermon "The Trouble with Submission." It is a sermon that I did not look forward to giving in that it is fraught with many difficult concepts. Yet, as I share in the sermon, I felt strongly that I needed to address the text and the topic in order to model for the congregation how someone with deep concerns for the passage, can engage the passage in a positive way.

Many of us in the mainline traditions have neglected to address the realities of family life from a biblical perspective. In the midst of our silence, the only voice that is offered comes from a more literal interpretation that provides clarity but offers a problematic guidance to modern family realities.

Scripture: Ephesians 5:21 – 6:9

"Be subject to one another out of reverence for Christ. Wives be subject to your husbands as you are to the Lord. For the husband is the head of the wife just as Christ is head of the church, the body of which he is Savior. Just as the church is subject to Christ, so also wives ought to be, in everything, to their husbands. Husbands, love your wives, just as Christ loved the church and gave himself up for her, in order to make her holy by cleansing her with the washing of water by the word, so as to present the church to himself in splendor, without a spot or wrinkle or anything of the kind – yes, so that she may be holy and without blemish. In the same way, husbands should love their wives as they do their own bodies. He who loves his wife loves himself. For no one ever hates his own body, but he nourishes and tenderly cares for it, just as Christ does for the church, because we are members of his body. For this reason a man will leave his father and mother and be joined to his wife, and the two will become one flesh. This is a great mystery, and I am applying it to Christ and the church. Each of you, however, should love his wife as himself, and a wife should respect her husband. Children obey your parents in the Lord, for this is right. 'Honor your father and mother' – this is the first commandment with a promise, 'so that it may be well with you and you may live long on the earth.' And, fathers do not provoke your children to anger, but bring them up in the discipline and instruction of the Lord. Slaves obey your earthly masters with fear and trembling, in singleness of heart, as you obey Christ; not only while being watched, and in order to please them, but as slaves of Christ, doing the will of God from the heart. Render service with enthusiasm, as to the Lord and not to men and women, knowing that whatever good we do, we will receive the same again from the Lord, whether we are slaves or free. And, masters, do the same to them. Stop threatening them, for you know that both of you have the same Master in heaven, and with him there is no partiality" (Ephesians 5:21 – 6:9, NRSV).

Sermon

I'm going to begin with some comments by Lewis Donelson after a sobering reading of scripture like that. I think he speaks for many of us. "We come at this point to one of the most controversial passages in Ephesians, and one of the most difficult for modern Christians. The controversy surrounds less what the passage means for that seems to be reasonably clear, but more what to do with this passage in modern Christian life. The analysis of family life that is given here which includes a clear pattern of dominance and submission does not square with many modern Christian perceptions of the ideal Christian family. Many Christians today insist that only some kind of egalitarian model in which power is equally distributed can properly inform the modern Christian family. But what we find in Ephesians is not egalitarian. We must admit that Ephesians argues for unequal distribution of authority even if that authority is exercised in a tender and loving way" (pp. 101-102).

I really think Donelson nails it on the head, at least in my reading of this scripture. This is a very difficult passage of scripture for a variety of reasons. One, we know our history. We know that scriptures like this have justified Christian slaveholders with having slaves--they simply quoted this text. The other issue is that if you were raised in a household like mine or you know conservative or evangelical folks, there are many who see these words as eternal moral precepts for every God-led family. This is God's model for the family. I think most of us would have a problem with that. I do. When I made mention of this passage this past week there were staff members who said, "Pastor Dave, why don't you just skip it?" Which is the mainline way of dealing with difficult passages. You just pretend it's not there.

I went to the lectionary, which is the three-year cycle of sermon topics for many mainline pastors, and this passage never appears in the three-year lectionary cycle. So my staff then asked me, "Why ARE you doing a sermon on this text?"

Well, there's a certain stubbornness in me that says if the lectionary doesn't want to cover it, I ought to at least attempt to tackle it. At least that was my thought on Tuesday, and by the time I got to Friday I began to waver a little bit. I had one staff person, when I mentioned that I was going to preach on why wives should submit to their husbands, physically react to the uttering of those words, literally almost pushing herself away from me. And I realize that this word 'submission' is a very, very powerfully loaded term, especially for women. So, I know that I am heading into terrain that is very, very difficult. Should we ignore this passage? Should we water it down so it is less explosive? Perhaps you have heard it explained this way. "Well slavery back in those days wasn't as bad as slavery was back in 19th century America." Folks, slavery is slavery – there's no way to water it down! How do thinking Christians really address and read difficult passages of scripture?

I am inspired by Phyllis Trible, who wrote a book a number of years ago called, *Texts of Terror* in which she takes four of the most difficult stories of the Old Testament and wrestles with them. She says, "I do this because I'm a Christian and they're in my sacred book the bible. I can't ignore them" (Trible, 1993). She doesn't try to redeem them; she doesn't try to justify them; she just simply says, "oh my", "oh my" and retells the story with all of its difficulty.

I'm hoping to provide a model for how we might look at and interpret difficult passages. I think this is vitally important not only as a discipline, but because I know a lot of evangelical brothers and sisters, who, still to this day in the 21st century, see this as a model for all Christ-centered families. There needs to be a deeper engagement with the text.

We're going to begin by simply looking at this text the way most scholars look at this text. These passages that were read today are called the *haustaflen*. It's German for "household rules." And it's in German because it was the German dudes who were thinking a lot about this stuff and so they got to name it first--*haustaflen*. These household rules appear in a differing variation in the Book of Colossians and there's smatterings of them in the Pastoral Epistles.

I find the *haustaflen* very difficult for a number of reasons. Those of you who have been a part of this series through Ephesians know that in Ephesians 2, Paul announced that Jesus revealed a mystery. Namely that the Gentiles were a part of God's plan and that God was in the process of bringing a new creation, a new human being where the distinctions between Jews and Gentiles would no longer have importance. We can almost hear the words of Paul in the book of Galatians where he says in our baptism there's no longer male nor female, slave nor free, Jew or Gentile – these are all gone, they've been transformed by Christ. In the last couple of weeks we've looked at our baptism and Paul has told us that in our baptism we are called to take off the old and to put on the new. All of this renewal and transformation seems to dominate Paul's worldview when all of a sudden, at the end of the book he places a bunch of rules that a secular Greco-Roman person would say, "Oh yeah, I can accept these. Yeah, I'm familiar with these rules, that's the way I run my family". In other words, the church borrowed them from the surrounding culture. And no one was saying, shouldn't there be a difference in the way Greco-Romans and Christians order their lives?

Since we can't call Paul up and interview him to find out exactly what was on his mind when he wrote all of these rules. But the story I'm telling is that in many ways Paul and the early church are trying to answer this question: how do we live our family life now that we're disciples? There wasn't a lot of modeling going on with Jesus. Remember what Jesus' disciples did with their families? They left them and followed Jesus for three years. When Jesus spoke about the family, what did he say? Biology doesn't count. Those who follow me are my brothers and sisters and my mother and father. (Luke 8:21). That's pretty radical stuff!

Then, in the first century, what did the church do? They eliminated the nuclear family and they all gathered together in a commune. That didn't last. And so it's Paul's attempt to try to address issues that are now happening years after Jesus' death and resurrection. In other words, everyone thought Jesus was coming again soon--He seems to be a bit delayed. Life has to go on, so the questioned-- what does it mean to be a disciple and to be a family member? And they, like we, assume certain social norms. These rules were those social norms. It is my belief that Paul takes these rules and he tries to massage them a little bit. If you're like me, you may thing he hasn't massaged them enough. But what I hope to do is to help you understand that he is trying to adapt this set of social norms and to put Christ in the center. And by doing that, hopefully we can glean some beneficial knowledge. I am not trying to justify these texts. I can't picture anybody who could them to justify slavery. I am not trying to justify these texts but I am trying to understand them, especially within their cultural milieu and to hear what the Spirit might say to us this day.

So, let's take a look to see what that Greco-Roman family structure of Paul's day was like. It was based upon an Aristotelian understanding of humanity. Aristotle believed that everyone was born into a certain status in life. So, if your father was a warrior, you would be a warrior. If your father was a carpenter, you would be a carpenter. If your father was a ruler, you'll be a ruler. You were born and nature dictated your particular lot in life. There was no vocational training in those days, other than the fact that you were going to learn the craft or the rules of the particular level of society into which you were born. If you were born male, there were certain rules and expectations. If you were born female there were certain rules and expectations. In that culture, if you were born male, you were in charge; if you were born female, you were there to raise families. If you were a child, you were expected to be obedient. In Paul's day there were assumptions that certain people were meant to be slaves and others were meant to be slave masters. And that's just the way it was. No one questioned it. In fact, to live a moral life in that day was simply to follow faithfully these norms of society.

So, Paul takes that, and he works with it a little bit. Again, from a 21st century point of view, I don't think he works with it enough. But, he's a first century person with a first century world view. We're 21st century people with a 21st century world view-- those are two vastly different worlds. I am not seeking to justify his world, I am seeking to understand his world and what he was trying to do with it. Paul takes those norms and he does three things with them that I think are uniquely Christian. First, he says that submission was to be defined by Jesus and not nature. Aristotle believed: wives should submit to their husbands, why? You are female. Nature dictates that you ought to be submissive. Paul says submission should be based upon Christ's example of submission, and notice in verse 21, he doesn't differentiate. He says, "Let us all submit to one another in reverence to Christ." He then offers an uneven comparison: "Wives submit to your husbands? Husbands, you love your wife". Paul's beginning words at least start to say that as Christians we know what true submission is because Christ models submission for us. It's almost as if Paul is saying, "wives submit to your husbands as Christ submitted himself to his disciples, to the world. Husbands love your wives as Christ has loved the church". In other words, Christ becomes the example for Christians to follow rather than the natural order of the world that simply says, do this because it's your lot in life.

The second thing that Paul does is he makes everyone have the power of agency. In that day, only men had the power of agency, the authority in the social structure. But Paul asked "wives, I ask that you be submissive to your husbands"; "children, I ask that you be obedient to your parents"; "slaves, I ask that you be obedient to your slave master." And then he took the one person who had agency and he qualified their agency. "Husbands, I want you to love your wives"; "parents I want you to nurture and instruct your children in the Lord"; and "slave masters I want you to treat your slaves as children of God." There is a sense that everyone is empowered to do these actions of their own volition, rather than dictated by nature.

The third thing Paul creates is a call for actions whose reference stands outside of the actor: so wives act in relation to husbands, husbands act in relation to wives, children act in relation to parents, parents to children, slaves to masters, masters to slave. Their instructions are to serve the other with a sense of compassion, care and nurture, rather than lording their authority over the other and expecting a groveling submission. There's not an abuse of the accepted hierarchy, there's still hierarchy. But within that hierarchy, there is an attempt to try to bring some kind of compassion and care and nurturing.

That of course is the Christ-like model. Christ has always said "I have come not be served but to serve" (Mark 10:45). That motto, that understanding of Christianity was never intended to allow people to walk on us, or to cause us to abandon our self-regard, but rather, to know who you are, willingly give yourself to one another. I think that is what Paul is saying. And we in the 21st century probably think he could have gone a lot further. Again, not to justify, but he was a man of his time, just like we are people of our time.

So what do we do with this? You've just had your bible study lesson for the day. What do we do with this? I just want to reiterate, from my perspective that this particular set of rules does not work in a modern-day family. I agree with Donelson. It seems to soften the edges, but guess what? It's still patriarchy; it's not egalitarian. There is not a sense of mutuality here. And so for me, this passage is not an eternal model for the family, it simply does NOT work! In fact, I've seen it lived out in very destructive ways. When I was a child, I can remember women being beaten by their drunk husbands and told from the scriptures, they just needed to "go back to their husband and submit more." So, I have too many examples of how bad these texts can become in real life; I'm going to preach against it, work through it, but I am not going to hang a sign on my house that these are the house rules.

That being said, I think I can learn something from this text. Donelson comments aren't we all culturally bound? He says, "The author's willingness to reinforce with Christian approval the patriarchal form of marriage and the dramatic inequalities of slavery is troublesome to modern Christians...We must remember that there is no such thing as pure Christianity untouched by its surrounding culture. Early Christianity makes no sense apart from its Jewish, and Greek and Roman culture. No one, no Christian, has ever stood outside of history. Christian ethics always lives in the moment of history in which it occurs. The author of Ephesians could not imagine life apart from the social structures of the ancient world. How could society exist without marriage, parents and slavery? The social possibilities available to us were not imaginable in the first century" (Donelson, pp. 106-107).

I think his words speak to us. While critiquing first century Christians, how does our 20th-21st century cultural milieu skew our understanding of the gospel? For example, look at our societal focus upon the individual rather than the community. Do you see anywhere in the scriptures where Jesus says, "I'm only just concerned about you"? Jesus always talks about how he dies for the world. And when Paul addresses Christians, he never addresses individuals, he always addresses the community. Paul, again in this text, uses the pronoun "you" which in English can be plural or singular, but the "you's" are all plural in our text. Our modern day culture dictates that one of the ways we hear the gospel is as individuals, untouched by anybody else. Yet such a concept is utterly alien to much of the bible; the biblical characters have no concept of the individual as we do. And so, when we infuse that individualism into the scripture, we are doing the same thing that the early church did with its understanding of slavery and the role of women and the role of children.

There is no possibility of me finding any application from this passage regarding slavery for our day. I acknowledge that forms of oppression and slavery exist around the world. But as far as this text goes there is no redeeming quality to slavery. I do think that this text has something that will help and inform us concerning a deeper understanding of marriage and child rearing I think in many ways, our Catholic brothers and sisters have held onto something that we too quickly jettisoned--that is to think of marriage as a sacrament, to see marriage as something spiritual. For many of us, marriage has been reduced to a contract between two autonomous individuals who are hoping with luck that they can make something with their life. We've sometimes lost the sense of the mystery of marriage. We see the image of Christ's relationship with the church enriching our understanding of how we live with one another. And along those lines, I think what we do here is we take these words of submission and love and proclaim that there is a mutuality here. It's not that husbands, you love, and wives, you submit--but rather husbands and wives please know that mutual love nurtures a relationship that includes a submissive love. What relationship will last 40 years with two people saying: "It's my way or the highway?" Mutuality might look like both husband and wife saying, "I have come to this moment because I love you and there are times I'm going to give and you know what, there are times when I know you are going to give, that's what love is about." Somehow, I think we've missed that. Maybe it is because of our fear of people who we have seen misuse the concept of submission as seen in this passage.

Someone asked me today If I had checked out with my wife concerning today's subject? No, I didn't. I didn't. But my 40 years of living with my wife have allowed me to understand how important it is to get this right--Because I love her. And I can't conceive of ever saying "I'm head of the household; you submit; you don't have a voice, sorry honey." That's not what has carried us through the years. So I do think, though, we have both bent, we have both given. We have both said, "I really want to do this particular action but I'm going to do this in light of our relationship". That's what I think a loving relationship is about. It's got to be mutual. And it's got to be loving.

The other thing I think we can learn from this text is that it assumes that parents will be very involved in the moral and Christian raising of their children, and that the raising and the nurturing will be loving. So that when parents do this, if it's done in love and it's done with care, that eventually children will come back and say, "I honor you. I honor you as a parent." It's hard for a 15-year-old to do that in the moment. That's where you've got to see the larger picture. There's sometimes when I might say, "Parents, there needs to be an adult in the room. There needs to be an adult in the room, and it needs to be a loving, caring adult who is not afraid of shaping and forming the life of their children." Our children long for that kind of love, because if you don't shape and form them, the culture will.

These words remind all of us as parents how important it is for us to offer love to our kids, a love that calls for active participation of their moral and spiritual development. Not just taking them to soccer, but active participation. Actively to love them and nurture them and care for them and give them those boundaries. Actively give them that sense of who they are, that they are Christians; that they are saved by God's grace. Actively show them that God loves them and God walks with them. Then you've got to let them go and you hope that at some point they turn around and say, "I honor you Mother. I honor you Father. You were everything I needed; at the time, and I didn't know it."

I'm going to end with these words from Lewis Donelson "For us then, our task is not to recreate the peculiar social structures found in the Bible, but to pursue Christian ethical principles as far as we can. Unfortunately, we have proven ourselves to be just as time-bound, culturally dominated, and self-protecting as the Christians who have gone before us. What is important is not to say that the author of Ephesians could have done better, although, he might well have done so. But to say that we must do better." And then he ends with these words: "Be subject to one another out of reverence for Christ" (p. 107).

I think they are words that I am going to be thinking about as I go forth from this place. Let's pause and reflect. Amen.

Chapter Sources

Donelson, Lewis. <u>Colossians, Ephesians, 1 and 2 Timothy, and Titus</u>. Westminster Bible Companion. Louisville, KY: Westminster John Knox Press. 1996.

Trible, Phyllis, (Speech heard in Des Moines, Iowa), 1993.

Chapter 11

A Defensive Struggle

Introduction

This is the last sermon in this short series on the Book of Ephesians. Paul ends his letter in a way that seems appropriate. He began Ephesians speaking of the cosmic dimensions of Christ, and now he ends with that same theme. As the sermon will make clear such themes for modern thinking Christians can seem a bit odd. This sermon seeks to acknowledge that uncomfortableness while still remaining with the text that is given.

Scripture: Ephesians 6:10-20

"Finally, be strong in the Lord and in the strength of his power. Put on the whole armor of God, so that you may be able to stand against the wiles of the devil. For our struggle is not against enemies of blood and flesh, but against the rulers, against the authorities, against the cosmic powers of this present darkness, against the spiritual forces of evil in the heavenly places. Therefore take up the whole armor of God, so that you may be able to withstand on that evil day, and having done everything, to stand firm. Stand therefore, and fasten the belt of truth around your waist, and put on the breastplate of righteousness. As shoes for your feet put on whatever will make you ready to proclaim the gospel of peace. With all of these, take the shield of faith, with which you will be able to quench all the flaming arrows of the evil one. Take the helmet of salvation, and the sword of the Spirit, which is the word of God. Pray in the Spirit at all times in every prayer and supplication. To that end keep alert and always persevere in supplication for all the saints.

Pray also for me, so that when I speak, a message may be given to me to make known with boldness the mystery of the gospel, for which I am an ambassador in chains. Pray that I may declare it boldly, as I must speak." (Ephesians 6:10-20, NRSV).

Sermon

This morning we conclude this short series of sermons centered on the book of Ephesians. This particular sermon has some very vivid imagery...the image of God's armor. As I was reflecting on this imagery, I realized that sometimes, as modern people, we have difficulty with biblical imagery in general.

I was thinking, and this has nothing to do with the sermon, that this is Christ the King Sunday. We as Americans have trouble with "kings," right? Recall that little Monty Python piece where the king comes galloping toward some common peasants and upon seeing the king they say, "You're not my king! I didn't vote for you. You don't vote for a king!" It's reflective of our discomfort with monarchs and regal images.

The concept of Christ the King Sunday is a bit difficult to hold on to because of that very modern understanding of "king." In much the same way, this text has some imagery that is a bit disturbing to people who are modern in their thinking. There's this talk about cosmic powers, about how there's a satanic presence all around us and there are all these rulers and things that are a part of the cosmos. I came across this image of such a reality (the sanctuary screen shows a picture of Jesus arm wrestling the devil) and I thought: "Yeah, I think that for some people that's how they picture this reality, much like an arm wrestle between Jesus and the devil." But that picture also speaks to me as to why our text today is a difficult passage; because most of us don't actually believe we are living in a world where there is a real devil. This seems to be a little archaic in our understanding. How can you be sure that there are cosmic forces all around us? We're rational, modern people. If we can't measure it and observe it, does it really exist?

In the same way, we may question biblical imagery such as this. The text is problematic, and this particular imagery has been used in a wrong way. For me, every time I read this passage, I see this image: crusaders--putting on the armor of God, and going out and slicing and dicing the evil people around them. We remember that there were many, many Christians who lived before us who did just that in a holy war against what was not Christian. They slaughtered thousands upon thousands of people, all in the name of Jesus. So this imagery includes realities like that as well.

Here's my advice when you have difficulty with biblical imagery. Be uncomfortable with your uncomfortableness. It's perfectly fine to be uncomfortable with some of this imagery. When it comes to this particular image that Paul uses to describe the powers of the air, maybe we can satisfy our modern prejudices. Prejudices that exist making us thing that because we are "modern" we actually think more clearly than people who lived long ago. Maybe we can simply admit to ourselves that even if we can't see it, measure it or observe it, it still could be possible. We might be able to affirm that there are forces of evil around us that transcend anything we can see. Paul seems to be utterly convinced of it. He began this book with that same kind of image, that Christ came to change the cosmos. It wasn't just "me and Jesus" for Paul. Jesus came to change everything, not just on earth, but in all of the universe. Paul ends the book with the sense that the battle hasn't been finished yet and that there is still a lot of reconciling ahead. The forces Paul recognizes are forces that transcend what we can see.

I don't know about you, but I have trouble with the notion of a personal devil. That doesn't mean that I don't think there is one, I just have problems with it. I have no trouble thinking about evil which goes well beyond any one particular person. And I do think at times we confront a kind of spirit of evil that can pervade a society and pervade the world. I believe that, but I know other people struggle with it, so just be comfortable with your struggle. But do be open to the idea that it might actually be possible.

And when it comes to those negative images, I think what we need to do [and this is my advice for anybody confronted by people who misinterpret a text] is to just dig deeper into the text. I mean, if we were to read this passage over and over again it would suddenly become obvious that a particular word appears over and over. The word is not "attack" or "annihilate," it's "stand." Stand. Stand. Stand. Stand. It's repeated four times. Stand. It's like, okay, you're getting it! Like the whole purpose of this armor is to stand, not to attack. It's defensive. It's so that I can stand firm in the faith. At least that's my reading of the text. Perhaps somehow you can see a more attack-oriented mode, but I don't see it. The first impression of the image can indeed take us there--to attack, I mean. Instead, when we go there, we need to just think "Oh wait, what about the text? Let me read the text more closely. What does it actually say? Oh, it says Stand, Stand." There's no sense of progress against evil, just simply, stand. Stand firm.

Why? Because God's going to deal with all that attacking stuff. I just need to stay faithful and true.

With that in mind, I think it's important for us to look at these passages and to dig a little deeper into what these passages might be saying. Our text starts with the word "finally." I just don't think this is an effective translation of the Greek. The Greek word has more of a sense of an eschatological tension, basically meaning "in the meantime" or "while time remains." Paul is a believer that we are the "in-between people"; that Christ has come, He has suffered and He has died. He rose again and He ascended into heaven and one day He will return. Presently, we sit in this "in-between time" and so while we're in this period, we need to remain firm--to stand against those powers that fight against us. I think somehow, the introductory word "finally'" misses it. It is akin to a speaker saying, "my final point is," rather than "we are standing in this eschatological tension between Christ's first coming and his second." So in the midst of this "in-between time," the way we stand is through two means.

The first is that we receive strength. Paul says: "Be strong in the Lord--Be strong in the Lord." He says it twice. He doesn't mean be strong in the Lord right now, as though you had received the sudden infusion of instant strength, nor does he mean finding the strength somewhere deep inside of you. If you read the text closely it says, "Be strong in the Lord." And because the Greek is in the present tense, it probably is better translated, "Be continually strong in the Lord"; be continually strong in the Lord every day, every hour, every minute. Just be continually strong. It's not like the power comes down and you get it--it's something that is always on-going; it's a process. So be strong in the Lord on an ongoing basis.

It should also be noted that the verb is in a passive voice, so it's not that there's some kind of strength that I need to find within me. It's something that comes from outside of me that I receive in a passive sense. God gives me this strength. So, one of the ways we stand is by standing strong in the Lord, because we have received the gift of strength that God gives us. We need this, according to Paul, because we are contending against the wiles of the devil. Another translation I love for this phrase is "the dirty tricks of the devil."

Paul is utterly convinced that if we are left to our own devices, our own strength, we will be annihilated by evil. The only way we can stand, our only hope, is to have the strength of God present in our lives. And so, to stand up against that kind of evil we need the strength that only God can give. That strength is lived out in putting on the armor of God. One of the things we need to be very aware of is that when we talk about such spiritual armor, we must remember that Paul is being very collective in his understanding. In other words, he's not calling for individuals to take on the armor, but for the church to take on the armor. Steven Fowl states "There is one further important point to make about this passage, it is very easy to read this discussion about the armor of God and then to assume that this is a set of instructions for individual believers to take up the armor. That is not really the way the text reads. Rather, the command to take up the armor of God is a summons to the community as a whole. Taking up the armor of God is a communal practice intricately tied to the unity of the church and the church's witness to the powers" (pp. 200-201).

It is the church that takes on the armor of God. This armor is fashioned after Roman soldiers because everybody in Ephesus had seen many Roman soldiers. They knew what a Roman soldier looked like. The meaning of the armor is infused by the words of Isaiah the prophet. If we were in a bible study, we would take a break and for the next half hour we would look at how every piece of armor is interpreted and infused by the prophet Isaiah.

One of the clear points from Isaiah is that the aspects of this armor, all of the characteristics, have little to do with human virtue, but rather are characteristics of God—righteousness, peace, and salvation. These are not human virtues. These are God characteristics. And so what Paul calls for the church to take on is God's armor, God's characteristics, as Isaiah has proclaimed them. Paul then begins to go through what this armor looks like. Almost every point he mentions from Isaiah can be identified in a corresponding reference point in the Book of Ephesians.

We begin with the Belt of Truth. Remember, Paul has said truth is not some kind of an abstract concept that we seek to discover, but what is truth? It is the way we live with one another. Speak the truth in love--be a community of truth. In other words, one of the ways the church defends against evil is that it is real. It is honest with itself and honest with each of its members; it's a community that has integrity. We all know integrity is one of the marks of anyone who is going to withstand great force.

We are all to take on the breast plate of righteousness. The Greek word there is *dikiaosune*. It comes from the Hebrew word *tsedheqa* and it can also be translated "justice." I like that translation better than righteousness. We wear the breast plate of justice. The church remains firm when it wears the justice of God. What does that look like? Care for the orphan, the widow, the poor, the marginal, the homeless, the foreigner, the outsider. The church becomes strong when it becomes that kind of community. It withstands evil; not by killing evil people, but by accepting the justice of God, by clothing itself in God's characteristics of justice.

We're also to put on shoes that allow our feet to run and share the message of peace. Remember, in chapter two, Paul defines this peace as an annihilation of a wall. A wall that separated Jews from Gentiles for centuries including all of the animosity that grew up around that wall. So, I would say that one of the ways the church addresses evil in the world is when it stands firm in its faith by engaging in the business of breaking down walls, calling people together who used to hate each other, and finding ways that they might connect in love.

Paul says this in Romans, don't return evil to evil people, but basically love them into guilt--love evil people to death (Romans 12:20-21). We are to be a people who proclaim a peace that doesn't build walls--it breaks down barriers.

We are also to be a people who have the shield of faith. We talked about this earlier when we considered Paul's understanding of faith discussed in chapter four. Faith is that which unites us--we are united in the faith. There's a unity in faith, but faith also is a basic trust that we have. These two aspects of faith provide a shield that defends us. And I like this imagery: faith protects us "from the fiery darts of the devil." What does that mean? Paul doesn't really say, but if you go to the Book of James, fiery darts are implied by James when he speaks of the power of the tongue to destroy people (James 3:1-12). So maybe we have the shield of faith to defend ourselves from our own inability, as a community, to speak the truth in love and to build one another up.

Faith helps us become a community that is shielded from all of the false notions, from all of the accusations, all of the diatribe that can be so destructive to community. These things bounce off and we are nurtured within the community that is surrounded by God's justice where we speak the truth in love and where we proclaim a gospel of peace.

We are also to wear the helmet of salvation. A helmet was both a protection and an identifier for a soldier and so when we proclaim the good news of salvation it identifies us as children of God.

And then, we are to take on the sword of the spirit which is the word of God. Many of us associate that phrase with the bible. I think that's a good assumption. I don't think we're right, though. I mean, it's a good assumption, but I don't think it's what Paul intended. When scripture talks about what we know as our bibles; it tends to use two words: *logos* which means "word", or *biblios*, which means "book." But Paul actually uses a different word here: *rehma*. And *rehma* is almost always talking about the spoken word. So for me, the sword of the Spirit is the sharing of the gospel; the speaking of the gospel. That also becomes a part of God's armor.

The fact of God's word being spoken is so clear throughout the Old Testament. When God speaks, He's not reading the bible. God speaks. And when He speaks, things happen, for example God's speech creates the world, according to Genesis 1. What is the one thing that drives King Saul crazy? He no longer hears a word from God. It isn't that he doesn't have his bible in front of him. No he's not hearing that life-giving speech of God. So, the arsenal we have is a proclamation of the gospel, the Good News. The church is a church that is able to stand up against evil when it proclaims good news, not rotten news, not vengeful news, not mean news. Good news. That's what overcomes evil and defends the faith.

Now, all of this is fueled by prayer. And if you look at your bibles, you will notice that the NSRV does a bad thing here. The translation committee decided that verse 18 should start a new paragraph. One gets the sense that prayer has nothing to do with what's preceded it. It's a new subject. But if you look at the Greek text, verses 18, 19, and 20 are all part of the same group of sentences. And so, prayer is very much involved. It's not that prayer is another part of the armor; prayer is the fuel. Prayer is the energy that allows the strength of God to work through us, so that the armor is fully functional.

Marcus Barth says that prayer becomes an expression of our whole life. He states 'The saints are encouraged·to offer their whole life and being as a prayer to God, whether they be active or passive, speaking or silent, whether they render a palpable service to Christ and their fellow human beings or share in the suffering of Christ and the world by bearing pain and misery and loneliness." (p. 806). I think he is exactly right. That which fuels the standing of the faithful is the giving of our lives. This giving of our life becomes a prayer. We just simply give ourselves to God and we know that we are clothed in the characteristics of God's armor. Not to annihilate evil, not to rid the world of evil, but simply to stand against the powers that work against a church which seeks to do the things that God is seeking to call the church to do.

It's easy to be on the offensive. We live in a culture that believes we ought to be on the offense. It's much more difficult to be a church that believes in peace and caring and compassion and kindness and welcome and the breaking down of walls. To be the kind of people God is calling the church in Ephesus to be requires a certain kind of internal integrity that is fueled by prayer, which then centers us in God's presence.

I promised myself to try to give you something practical at the end of each of these sermons. So this week I came up with something and I don't know if it's any good or not, but it is practical. One of the things I began to think about was taking the importance of standing firm too far. There's a thin line between standing firm and just being flat-out stubborn. You see, I'm a stubborn person, so I really know what that's like. It's a hard line to discern because sometimes you think you're standing firm and you're just being obstinate; you're just being stubborn.

Pastor Archie Smith writes about this issue: "There's a difference between being stubborn and standing firm. Paul is not asking us to be stubborn, wedded to an opinion rooted in prejudice, or close-minded, but he is asking us to stand in something that is not transient; something that is transcendent and renewing. This means being willing to be humble and to risk being unpopular, even to suffer ridicule if not worse, as a faithful person in the community of faith. A stubborn person will not listen to ideas that are different from his or her own. A stubborn posture rejects alternatives out of hand and refuses regardless of the situation to change one's position. Stubbornness is not self or other discerning; it is not informed, and it does not grow. It is enshrined in a closed circle of certainty and becomes fearful, boisterous and one-dimensional...The stubborn heart and mind are impervious to reason and may constitute the one way to hide insecurity. Standing firm is different. Standing firm means that one is willing to debate, listen and consider alternatives in order to reach a beneficial goal, while at the same time not sacrificing basic principles. Martin Luther King, Jr. stood firm on non-violence. Nelson Mandela stood firm and resolute against apartheid. All stood firm against injustice. The lesson we draw from them is that having a strong ego means demonstrating an equally powerful concern for justice and compassion, which are to be grounded in the convictions of the community and open to critical evaluation" (pp. 374,376).

This is how we stand firm. If only the church had read this passage a little better--that our calling is not to slice and dice the enemy, but to stand firm. And that firmness is not a matter of being closed and stubborn. It's a sense of confidence, and being in God's presence and in doing that, we are open to dialogue, and change, and different perspectives because we're standing firm. I know so many people who want to defend Jesus--well I think Jesus can defend Himself. We need to stand firm in the faith, and that firmness is one of confidence, that I may be wrong, and you might be right. It is a perspective that says "You know what? We can work this all out because we're standing firm in the faith, not fighting over the faith."

I think that's a good way to end, don't you? So this week, that's your job. I want you to practice standing firm and not being stubborn. Have someone who loves you be the judge at the end of the week and see how well you did. Stand firm! Stand firm! Stand firm! Amen

Chapter Sources

Barth, Markus. Ephesians 4-6. (The Anchor Bible). Garden City, New York: Doubleday and Company, 1974.

Fowl, Stephen. Ephesians. (The New Testament Library). Louisville, KY: Westminster/John Knox Press, 2012.

Smith, Archie. "Ephesians 6:10-20" in Feasting on the Word, Year B, Volume 3. Louisville, KY: Westminster John Knox Press, 2009.

CPSIA information can be obtained
at www.ICGtesting.com
Printed in the USA
FSHW010003080620
70936FS